# When Not If:
## Surrogacy for Australians

Stephen Page

THIS BOOK IS WRITTEN ON THE LANDS OF THE TURRBAL AND JAGERA PEOPLES.

TO MY HUSBAND MITCHELL AND TO MY CHILDREN

THIS BOOK IS DEDICATED TO THE THOUSANDS OF PEOPLE THAT I'VE HELPED BECOME PARENTS – AND THEIR CHILDREN, AND ABOVE ALL TO SURROGATES – THE EXTRAORDINARY WOMEN WHO HELP OTHERS ACHIEVE THE DREAM OF PARENTHOOD.

# Contents

1. DISCLAIMER ................................................................. v
2. ABOUT ME – MY PROFESSIONAL JOURNEY ......... 1
3. ABOUT ME – MY PERSONAL JOURNEY ................ 31
4. WHEN NOT IF ............................................................ 59
5. DEATH – THE FIRST REASON YOU WON'T BECOME A PARENT ................................................. 65
6. YOU WON'T GET THERE – GIVING UP .................. 69
7. THE THIRD REASON YOU WON'T GET THERE - MONEY ...................................................................... 73
8. THE FOURTH REASON FOR GIVING UP – NOT USING A DONOR ....................................................... 79
9. JARGON SCHMARGON .............................................. 81
10. WHAT ABOUT ADOPTION? ....................................... 93
11. HOW NUMBERS DON'T LIE – OVERSEAS OR DOMESTIC? ............................................................... 97
12. LEGAL ISSUES ABOUT GOING OVERSEAS ........ 105
13. FINDING A SURROGATE .......................................... 115
14. SURROGACY FOR RAINBOW INTENDED PARENTS- AND OTHER DISCRIMINATION ........ 121
15. CHOOSING AN IVF CLINIC ..................................... 137
16. THERE ARE GUARANTEES AND GUARANTEES 141
17. WHO WANTS TO BE PARENTS THROUGH SURROGACY? ........................................................... 145
18. WHO WANTS TO BE A SURROGATE? ................................................................ 147
19. THE RIGHT TO KNOW ............................................. 153
20. CHOOSING A SURROGACY AGENCY V. A BOTTLE OF MILK .................................................................... 159

| | | |
|---|---|---|
| 21. | SURROGACY IN THE AUSTRALIAN CAPITAL TERRITORY | 163 |
| 22. | SURROGACY IN THE NORTHERN TERRITORY | 169 |
| 23. | SURROGACY IN NEW SOUTH WALES | 171 |
| 24. | SURROGACY IN QUEENSLAND | 177 |
| 25. | SURROGACY IN SOUTH AUSTRALIA | 183 |
| 26. | SURROGACY IN TASMANIA | 189 |
| 27. | SURROGACY IN VICTORIA | 195 |
| 28. | SURROGACY IN WESTERN AUSTRALIA | 225 |
| 29. | INTERSTATE ARRANGEMENTS | 233 |
| 30. | SURROGACY ISSUES FOR AUSTRALIANS LIVING OVERSEAS | 235 |
| 31. | PLAYING NICELY WITH OTHERS | 237 |
| 32. | A CALL FOR CHANGE | 239 |

# DISCLAIMER

The description by me in this book of laws and their application is intended by me to be a general description only, and is not intended to be specific advice in the personal circumstances of individuals who have not retained me or my firm. I don't know what your journey is, and the legal issues specific to you, unless you have engaged me. ALWAYS GET EXPERT LEGAL ADVICE FIRST before taking any action in your journey to become parents through surrogacy. The law in this area is new, uncertain and often untested. I have had to dig too many parents (and some surrogates) out of holes of their own making, or where they have obtained less than ideal legal advice. As Alexander Pope said: "A little learning is a dangerous thing." By all means, use this book to help guide you on your journey- but get expert legal advice before you decide to do anything.

If you want me to help you on your journey to parenthood, then contact me: +61 7 3221 9751

or [stephen@pageprovan.com.au](stephen@pageprovan.com.au). I will be able to help you once I am retained.

When Not If: Surrogacy for Australians

Copyright © Stephen Page

First published: 2022

ISBN: 978-0-6456063-3-1 Paperback

ISBN: 978-0-6456063-4-8 e-Book

All rights reserved. Without limiting the rights under copyright reserved above, no part of this publication may be reproduced, stored in or introduced into a database and retrieval system or transmitted in any form or by any means (electronic, mechanical, photocopying, recording or otherwise) without the prior written permission of the owner of the copyright.

Published with the assistance of Angel Key Publications P/L

https://angelkey.com.au

CHAPTER 1

# ABOUT ME – MY PROFESSIONAL JOURNEY

The greatest honour in my life has been to help others achieve parenthood. When my clients share the happy news and pictures of their new born babies, I invariably cry tears of joy. I have always empathized with others who have struggled to become parents. I am so lucky to do this work. I knew since about the age of 4 or 5 that I wanted to be a dad. What I didn't know was that I would face infertility nor that I would undertaken my own surrogacy journey - but I cover that issue in **Chapter 2.** This chapter is about my professional journey with surrogacy.

Somehow, I have become the leading fertility and surrogacy lawyer in Australia. I've been asked many times how that happened, including what drew me to surrogacy and fertility law.

By the end of 2021 I had advised (by my estimate) in over 1,750 surrogacy journeys since 1988, plus hundreds of other clients seeking to become parents through sperm, egg and embryo donation or other form of assisted reproductive treatment, such as posthumous use. This book focuses on surrogacy.

As of the end of 2021, my clients have come from every part of Australia – all the big cities such as Sydney, Melbourne, Brisbane and then places of few people – the Outback, Pilbara, WA Wheatbelt, rural South Australia, Wagga Wagga, Byron Bay – you name it. My clients have come from the southernmost parts of Australia, in Hobart to the northernmost- in Darwin and north of Cairns.

In addition, I have acted for clients who live overseas. As of the end of 2021, I have advised clients living in 34 countries overseas concerning either surrogacy or assisted reproductive treatment:

## America
- Brazil
- Canada
- United States of America

## Europe
- Belgium
- Denmark
- Germany
- France
- Italy
- Ireland
- Luxembourg
- Netherlands
- Poland
- Russia
- Spain
- Switzerland
- Ukraine
- United Kingdom

## Middle East
- Israel
- United Arab Emirates

## Asia
- China
- Hong Kong
- India
- Indonesia
- Japan
- Malaysia
- Philippines
- Singapore
- South Korea
- Thailand

## Oceania

- New Caledonia
- New Zealand
- Papua New Guinea
- Solomon Islands
- Samoa

I studied law in Brisbane. When I went to university, family law did not interest me at all. I could never have imagined that my professional career would be devoted to family law, and through it, to fertility law. I could never imagine doing that kind of work. I was interested in the intellectual nature of trusts.

I was annoyed when I got 79% for Equity (which included trusts) that I did not get the prize. Someone got 80%.

I remember, as students do, one student raising legal issues about when life begins. I thought it all so theoretical and not connected with reality that of course I would never have to do anything with that. What I didn't know then was that my career would take me to that very point.

My first surrogacy client was in 1988. By that stage, I had been working in fulltime legal practice for about three years and as a solicitor for just over a year. To my amazement a woman came into my office, advising that she had given birth. She said that she had become a surrogate for a husband and wife. I had heard of the word "*surrogate*" only in passing because there had been recent legislation about that. She had, by necessity, undertaken traditional surrogacy, not gestational (which I'll talk about later) and was therefore the genetic mother. She said that she had been paid $10,000 by this couple to have the baby. Her question of me was:

> *"Can I keep both the money and the baby?"*

It is funny that after all these years I can still remember those words. I was shocked that someone could be so callous. I can still remember the precise words that formed in my brain in shock, reacting to her statement.

I immediately thought of the pain that the couple were going through – that they had to rely on someone else to become parents and here she was holding over their child (but also her genetic child). My advice was:

*"Yes, you can".*

In reaction to the first court case about surrogacy (the Baby M case in 1987 in New Jersey[1]) all the Australian States had considered laws about surrogacy. Only Queensland had passed a law which banned *all* surrogacy, commercial or not, traditional or gestational, inside or outside Queensland – if undertaken by Queenslanders. Because of what the surrogate and the intended parents had done, the surrogacy journey was illegal. As it was an illegal contract, it was void (and the *Surrogate Parenthood Act 1988* (Qld) specifically said that). The money therefore lay where it fell. Because she had been paid the money, she could keep it.

And the baby? If the matter ever got to the Family Court, chances were that because she was the mother and had this bond with her child from birth, she would be successful in the court[2]. But the chances were that the matter would never go to court. This was because the intended parents would be reluctant to go to court when there was a risk that as a result they could be prosecuted.

The matter never went to court. I don't know whether that child (if they are still alive) has ever been told the truth about their conception.

From the beginning of my legal practice, I did a lot of domestic violence work. I had never been exposed to domestic violence in my life and was shocked about how some husbands treated their wives. Since then, sadly, I've seen domestic violence by wives to their husbands, in LGBTIQ+[3] relationships, and then family violence, for example, from sons to their mothers. Domestic violence seems to be a never ending part of family law in Australia. I hope one day it ends. I have played my part in seeking to end domestic violence, but that is another story, for another day.

In this period in the 1990's, I met a remarkable woman, Vic Ogilvy. Vic had just come out of a marriage with a man and came out of the closet. She was then a domestic violence worker. We worked closely together. She, like me, was and is passionate about helping others and stopping domestic violence. One Friday afternoon in about 1992 she called me out of the blue and said that there was a presentation in an hour or so about lesbians and family law and the speaker, another solicitor, had pulled out. Could I speak?

Wanting to help, I readily agreed, not knowing what I was going to talk about. In those days, lesbians were often discriminated in the Family Court about parenting. It was a disgraceful turn of events I thought that parents would be discriminated against under the law, not based on the quality of their parenting but based on their sexuality. I have always felt passionate that one of the foundations of our democratic society is that all are equal under the law. I turned up. There were about 30 women there and one man, me.

It went well. I started talking about how the law at times then discriminated against lesbians in parenting, and how they were not recognized if they were couples when they had kids or had property. Many had left husbands- and I started talking about domestic violence by some Australian men to their wives. When I started talking about some of the common putdowns and swear words used by these men to their wives, one woman- with tears welling up in her eyes- said:

*"That's what my husband did to me. I didn't realise it was domestic violence."*

Over time I met many lesbian clients. A feature of assisting lesbians as clients has been to help them become parents, including navigate some of the nightmares of the legal system. My fertility practice in reality started from that seminar where I was the fill in guest. I'm glad I went.

Over time, I started acting for more and more clients seeking to start their parenting journey. Intended parents would then consult me about how to become parents through surrogacy. At first, this would be a very quick meeting. Following formal introductions, after a minute or so, I would say[4]:

*"For you to undertake any form of surrogacy here or anywhere else is an offence."*

I would then be asked:

*"Well, where can we do it lawfully?"*

Given my duty to my clients, I had to look it up. This wasn't easy. The internet was, to put it politely, in its formative stages. I had to look at dusty law books. The result? I could give advice to clients about where they could move to, in order to become parents[5]. I then became aware of the law in each state and territory in Australia- all eight systems of law, that my interstate colleagues would not have done. A lawyer in Sydney would have focussed on the law there, and a lawyer in Melbourne would have focused on the law there. Because Queensland criminalised all forms of surrogacy, I was forced out of duty to my clients to find out the law everywhere else in Australia.

And I have kept up to date ever since.

What that taught me was that intended parents were desperate to have children, and that any prohibition on surrogacy does not work. Intended parents will go somewhere else in order to pursue the dream of parentage. Surrogacy ought to be regulated ( and anyone who say there aren't any ethical issues with surrogacy is either a fraud or a fool, or both), but as I said prohibition doesn't work. In this the words of Sir David Attenborough ring true. He was standing beside an albatross when he said this in *The Trials of Life* (1990):

> *"If you watch animals objectively for any length of time, you're driven to the conclusion that their main aim in life is to pass on their genes to the next generation. Most do so directly, by breeding. In the few examples that don't do so by design, they do it indirectly, by helping a relative with whom they share a great number of their genes. And in as much as the legacy that human beings pass on to the next generation is not only genetic but to a unique degree cultural, we do the same. So animals and ourselves, to continue the line, will endure all kinds of hardship, overcome all kinds of difficulties, and eventually the next generation appears."*

That last sentence, of enduring all kinds of hardship and overcoming all kinds of difficulties, describes the complexities and difficulties of those who undertake surrogacy. Surrogacy is of course the most complex way of having a baby.

And then Australia saw what I had been seeing. Following then Senator Stephen Conroy and his wife Paula Benson's inability to undertake surrogacy[6] in their home state of Victoria, due to the laws of Victoria which made their surrogacy journey there virtually impossible and instead went to New South Wales in order to become parents, then federal Attorney-General Philip Ruddock called on each of the states to legislate about surrogacy. Within a short timeframe, all the states did so. Across Australia, laws were passed to enable the legalisation and regulation of altruistic surrogacy and the criminalisation of commercial surrogacy. Sadly, these laws remain inconsistent.

Of all the States, Queensland had the most vicious debate of all, with the passage of what became the *Surrogacy Act 2010* (Qld). The Bligh Government (ALP) was insistent that the Act include gays, lesbians and singles. The then LNP Opposition, in what was a conscience vote on both Bills, came up with its Bill which was *identical* to the Government Bill, except it excluded gays, lesbians and singles and proposed to criminalise them for seeking to become parents through surrogacy.

I was outraged. In my view, the law should apply equally. I then blogged about it, wrote about it in my then column in Brisbane gay paper QNews, and spoke to every media that I could. I was only one voice, but I wanted to make that voice count. The principle of democracy after all is that all of us are equal under the law; but here was a proposal to deny rights granted to others, based on sexuality or relationship status. For me it was never an issue about party affiliation, but about the issue itself.

I was particularly outraged at the conduct of then Opposition Shadow Attorney-General Lawrence Springborg. Labor member Grace Grace had invited LGBTIQ+ members of the community to the Parliament. This was a non-partisan event and, looking back, historic. I was among the group who met politicians from all sides, including Ministers, the Opposition Leader John-Paul Langbroek and opposition frontbenchers. I was hoping that LGBTIQ+ issues were no longer a party political affair.

I remember that Lawrence Springborg was there and he left the formal event. I thought nothing of it. Politicians live extraordinarily busy lives.

Afterwards there was a barbecue for the event at Parliament House. To my surprise, Lawrence Springborg reappeared - where he worked the room, shaking hands and being friendly and chatty.

Where had he been during the break? It turns out that he had been to see the Parliamentary Counsel to draft his Bill which was identical to the Government's Surrogacy Bill – but to criminalise gays, lesbians and singles undertaking surrogacy. He did not have the decency or honesty to tell the LGBTIQ+ people at the barbecue of his conduct[7].

The Government Bill was enacted.

By 2010, when Queensland passed the *Surrogacy Act 2010* (Qld) and other States enacted similar law, I saw light on the horizon. Luckily there was a new dawn by which intended parents could be parents.

In 2011 I spoke at the first International Surrogacy Conference – organised by the American Bar Association, in Las Vegas.

Following that conference, I became an international representative on the Assisted Reproductive Treatment Committee of the American Bar Association. I remain in that position. Between 2012 and 2016 I had the honour of steering through the 400,000 plus membership of the American Bar Association a policy concerning a proposed Hague Convention on international surrogacy arrangements[8]. Work on this policy took up hundreds if not thousands of unpaid hours of my time. I lost count of the number of emails and meetings involved to steer this through. The policy was primarily written by Bruce Hale[9], a colleague from Boston, and me. Throughout there was the unflinching support, hard work and wise words of the then chairs of the ART Committee, colleagues Steve Snyder[10] from Minneapolis, Rich Vaughn[11] from Los Angeles and future chair Dean Hutchison from Boston[12]- and many other attorneys in the US and elsewhere. It was a joint effort by every means. I was deeply honoured that I was given the responsibility as an outsider- a non-American, to steer this through.

Since 2011 the Hague Conference on Private International Law[13], which writes Hague Conventions[14] and of which Australia has been a proud member for many years, has had a project about writing a convention concerning international surrogacy arrangements. Fortuitously, any convention or protocol is likely to be along the lines of what I was advocating through the American Bar Association, which is to recognise parenthood when there has been a court order in the other country (by which parenthood is established for intended parents who have undertaken surrogacy).

I have always believed that a convention would be a good thing, as there is a lack of international law concerning surrogacy. It would be good to give parents and their children certainty about their status, and make the journey home so much easier- wherever they go. Parents after all should be recognized as parents of their children, and their children should be recognised as their children. Parents should not be legal strangers to their children[15]. I was concerned as to the model of a convention suggested by some academic commentators would make a nightmare of any international journey and make it nigh on impossible. Lawyers like me who had feet on the ground, helping actual clients on actual parentage journeys, took a view opposed to that model.

A Hague Convention is still watch this space. Regrettably, differences between countries' approaches has made having a practical convention still a thing of the future rather than a here and now.

When I spoke at that conference in Las Vegas[16], I asked the 200 odd lawyers (mainly American) there:

*"Does anyone have a case on conception? Our Surrogacy Act says that a surrogacy arrangement must be signed before 'the child was conceived' but does not define conception. I'm afraid of having a Catholic judge who might define conception as the act of fertilisation, not the act of pregnancy."*

The response was universal:

*"No we don't. That sounds really interesting. Let us know how you go."*

In 2012 I was fortunate to appear in a court case in Brisbane that was the first in the world about what is conception i.e. when does life begin[17].

I was fortunate to act for the surrogate. My submissions – that conception was the act of pregnancy, not fertilisation - were accepted by the court. When you are doing the first of your kind in the world, you have to think differently, but because it was a court case, not leave anything to chance. My submissions on the point were not short. But they left nothing to chance. The judge described the baby as a *"miracle of modern medicine"* and of course her Honour was right[18].

Subsequently, Anna Bligh as Premier of Queensland was dumped and Campbell Newman elected in a landslide. I knew from previous dealings that Campbell Newman was not a homophobe[19]. Nevertheless, his Government started winding back protections for LGBTIQ people.

In 2012 I was in the United States to speak at a conference. On the way back, I stopped off in Las Angeles to meet a leading surrogacy lawyer, Andy Vorzimer. We had worked together but never met. When I saw Andy and said: *"G'day"*, Andy greeted me with the words:

> *"Why is Queensland cracking down on gays and lesbians doing surrogacy?"*

I responded that there were changes to the civil partnership laws. He corrected me. While I was overseas, the then LNP Attorney-General Jarrod Bleijie[20] announced in Parliament that the Government was considering amending the *Surrogacy* Act to put it back to what Lawrence Springborg wanted – which was to strip away the recognition of the non-birth mother in a lesbian relationship (making Queensland out of step with everywhere else in Australia) and to criminalise gays, lesbians and singles undertaking surrogacy.

I immediately decided to fight the change, although I thought the prospect of success in resisting the change was somewhere between 0 and 3%. I thought that the odds were so low because I could not imagine that the Attorney-General would have said what he had said without it having been discussed at Cabinet, and because the Newman Government had a huge majority. It could enact pretty well anything it wanted.

I was told that it was *"foolish"* and *"brave"* for me to take on the Government. I countered with that if I did not do so, I would be seen as *"weak"* and *"cowardly"*, because I did more of this work than anyone else, and if I did not stand up against this proposal, who would?

It was important to put a line in the sand for what I thought was morally wrong. I never thought that my actions would ever have an impact on my personal life, in the sense of affecting whether or not I could be a parent. I was already a dad: see **chapter 2**. To my amazement, I became the convenor of Queenslanders for Equality, which spearheaded opposition to the change – in direct opposition to the Australian Christian Lobby.

Queenslanders for Equality had a huge membership of seven. We had a launch of a petition on a Sunday by then opposition leader Anastasia Palaszczuk and her deputy Jackie Trad. Following the launch, the seven of us went for lunch. Stupidly, I said:

"Who's in charge after today?"

I then found out I was!

It was an all-out fight which I did in my spare time. After nine months of this, of the seven original members, there were only two of us left – Phil and me. Phil said to me that he had burnout and couldn't go on anymore. I couldn't blame him. He, like me had put his heart and soul into the fight. The fight seemed all consuming. Nothing seemed to change. Our fight seemed hopeless. His email to me was sent on the Monday in 2013. After receiving his email, I was immediately depressed. I felt the weight of the world upon my shoulders – that it was just me against the might of the Government.

My mood changed three days later. A media report was that the Government had "*deferred*" the proposal. It was dead in the water. Thankfully, the laws did not become enacted. Anyone, irrespective of their sexuality and relationship status, could be parents.

During that period I was fortified by my clients who would otherwise have been discriminated against. I particularly recall a client who was the mother of the intended mother. My client was the surrogate. Originally her daughter and son-in-law were to be the parents, but just before they were to sign up to the deal, he got cold feet:

"I don't want you. I don't want this marriage. I don't want to be a parent. I don't want to go through surrogacy. I'm going home to mother."

And did.

The daughter and her parents were determined to proceed. Ultimately a beautiful baby girl was born and a parentage order made.

During the course of their journey, this political debate raged. I pointed out to my client that under the proposal, what she and her husband were doing for their daughter would be illegal, resulting in each of them possibly receiving a maximum penalty of up to 3 years imprisonment. My client, a feisty Italian woman, responded:

*"Governments don't play God. They don't tell us when we can and can't have children."*

Sadly, that was not the end of the fight for recognition. Intended parents who underwent surrogacy overseas were left with a mess. As seen in chapter 10, only about 1 in 5 children born via surrogacy to Aussies are born in Australia. The rest are born overseas. We are great at exporting our intended parents. However, these same intended parents were recognised as parents of their children for the purposes of citizenship – but not recognised as parents for family law and inheritance. This was an absolutely crazy position, but the one that they faced. When I talked of this Las Vegas in 2011, my international colleagues thought that we Australians were nuts. How could I disagree? The position was illogical, and harmful for the children.

I thought of a number of ways around this. In some places in the United States where second parent adoptions occur as part of the surrogacy journey (such as Hawaii or Minnesota) the adoptive parent was a parent as a matter of law in Australia. So more of my clients went there, where it would mean at least one of them would be recognised as a parent.

I also thought of another workaround which was that if a court order was made in the United States to recognise someone as a parent, then if that order could be registered in Australia with the

Family Court of Australian, then they would be recognised here too. Our *Family Law Act* 1975 (Cth) - which deals with divorces and arrangements for children - allows for the recognition of overseas child orders, if they are made in the right place. The right place turns out to be most of the US[21]. There were subsequently six cases in the Family Court, of which I was on the record for five[22]. In the other case, the lawyers' names can't be published[23]. The first three cases were successful, the last two were not because the judge took the view that she could not exclude commercial surrogacy and in the exercise of her discretion and with no risk factors to the child, declined to register the order. The judge based her decision out of concerns that Parliament had legislated to make commercial surrogacy illegal.

The situation became crazy in 2017 with a decision by three judges in the Family Court[24] in which the court declined to find that a couple who had lived in Victoria and undertaken surrogacy in India, were the parents and that it was unlikely that the surrogate was a parent either. The Court did not look at the elephant in the room: if the intended parents were unlikely to be the parents, and the surrogate was unlikely to be a parent, who was? As a matter of public policy, someone should be a child's parent. I told The *Australian* that the decision was *"nuts"*. It seems little regard was had to the *International Convention* on the *Rights of the Child* whereby the best interests of the child needed to be taken into account[25] and the child had a right to an identity[26].

Thankfully, in 2019 the High Court came along[27] and decided in a non-surrogacy case, that who is a parent under the *Family Law Act* is someone seen in the wider view of Australian society to be a parent. Thankfully, intended parents who undertake surrogacy overseas will normally be seen as the parents for the purposes of Australian law.

In March 2020, I went into shock as everyone else did about the spread of Covid-19. For a short time, IVF was banned in Australia. Thankfully after a short period it resumed. Australia, alone in the world apart from North Korea, banned its citizens and residents from travel overseas, except for humanitarian reasons. Suddenly the plans of many intended parents to go overseas to be at the births of their children were disrupted.

At first the approach by the Government was *ad hoc*, inconsistent, confused and chaotic. Those seeking to go overseas had to apply to the government for permission- but no one knew how it was going to work. Permissions were refused repeatedly- or granted for spouses on the same flight- but granted days apart. Flights were cancelled left, right and centre. Eventually, only one airline flew directly between Australia and North America. United Airlines[28], to its credit, kept up daily flights between Sydney and LAX. At a time when Qantas should have been celebrating its 100th birthday, it stopped flying international flights for the first time ever. Not even during World War II did that happen.

I decided to do four things to help:

1. I wrote to Peter Dutton and pointed out that Australian intended parents going to the US and Canada for surrogacy invariably relied on the child's US and Canadian passports to fly home, along with an Electronic Travel Authority (ETA) issued online by the Australian Government. They did so because an ETA could be obtained in 10 minutes, whereas obtaining Australian citizenship in the US and Canada would take 2 to 4 months. I was very concerned that because the Government had stopped issuing ETA's that parents and kids would be stuck, and at high risk of getting Covid. A bureaucrat wrote back to me that the policy was for Australian citizenship to be obtained over there.

Nevertheless there was a marked change in approach. Shortly after that, processing times for Australian citizenship in the US and Canada for children born via surrogacy dropped from 2 to 4 months to 1 to 5 business days! It has stayed there ever since. Let's see if it remains there now that ETA's have issued again.

2. To share as much information as possible with my colleagues in the US, Canada and elsewhere, and others such as travel agent Craig Fyfe[29], and work as collaboratively as possible. **See Chapter 30- playing nicely with others**.
3. I convened a group of Australians concerned with surrogacy, including Sam Everingham from Growing Families[30] and

Roman Deauna from Far and Wide Migration[31], to ensure that our information was up to date, so that any approaches we took for clients was as helpful as possible

4. I promised to my clients that I would move heaven and earth if needed to get them there, and to get them and their babies back. This promise included making representations to MP's. Some, like Scott Morrison's office, were very helpful. Others were not. I kept my promise. I was aided in this particularly challenging time by my then associate Dharma Gan. All my clients got over and all and their babies came back.

Thankfully the madness of international travel during the Covid restrictions seems finally to be at an end.

In the meantime, I have made submissions to surrogacy and or ART reviews in Tasmania (2012), New South Wales (2014), House of Representatives (2015, 2016)[32], South Australia (2016, 2018, 2019), Western Australia (2018) and Victoria (2018). In 2021 I was a member of the Northern Territory government's surrogacy joint working group. Hopefully the Top End will have surrogacy laws before long. I am proud, for example, that South Australian authorities listened to me and ensured that there was greater protection of surrogates there (2015), removal of discrimination in surrogacy against same sex couples (2017), and that the *Surrogacy Act 2019* (SA) specifically takes up three issues I advocated for: the removal on the requirement that intended parents had to undertake IVF in South Australia- so intended parents have freedom to choose their doctor and clinic, that surrogates have bodily autonomy[33] and that the human rights of all (including the surrogate, intended parents and the child) have to be taken into account[34].

During the course of my career, I have been fortunate to speak and write about surrogacy around the world, including for the:

- International Bar Association
- International Academy of Family Lawyers
- International Family Law Journal
- International Federation of Gynecologists and Obstetricians (FIGO)

- Academy of Adoption and Assisted Reproduction Attorneys
- American Society for Reproductive Medicine
- Royal College of Australia and New Zealand Obstetricians and Gynecologists
- Canadian Fertility and Andrology Society
- Fertility Society of Australia and New Zealand
- Family Court of Australia
- Queensland Law Society
- Family Law Section of the Law Council of Australia
- Women Judges Association of Australia
- Family Law Practitioners Association of Western Australia
- Law Society of South Australia
- Hunter Valley Family Law Association
- North Queensland Law Association
- Miller du Toit Cloete/University of Western Cape South African family law conference.

Way back in 1996 I obtained Queensland Law Society accredited family law specialisation, which I have now been recognised by the Society for holding for 25 years.

On the same day in September 2014 I was accepted as a Fellow of the International Academy of Family Lawyers, the most prestigious group of family lawyers in the world and the first non-US or Canadian attorney of what is now the Academy of Adoption and Assisted Reproduction Attorneys. I am now a member of the IAFL's Parentage, LGBT, and Forced Marriage Committees.

I have been fortunate to be a guest lecturer at Hong Kong University, the University of the Western Cape and Monash University. Since 2017 I have lectured in Ethics in the Law and Reproductive Medicine in the Masters of Reproductive Medicine course at the University of New South Wales. I was fortunate in 2019 to receive an award for excellence in teaching from the University.

The number of presentations that I have done is embarrassingly long and can be seen on my website: www.pageprovan.com.au.

I have presented at conferences throughout Australia and the world, in Australia including Townsville, Brisbane, Gold Coast, Port Stephens, Sydney, Canberra, Hobart, Adelaide, Melbourne and Margaret River. I am yet to present in the Northern Territory.

Overseas, I have presented at conferences in London, Cape Town, Phnom Penh, Hong Kong, Anchorage, San Francisco, Chicago, Las Vegas, Nassau (Bahamas), Denver, Charleston and Cape Town, among others.

*When I took a walk in the afternoon on one of the days of the American Academy of Adoption Attorneys/American Academy of Assisted Reproduction Attorneys in Charleston in 2013, I was surprised by these locals, who dressed in the manner of the Old South.*

*Speaking at the Miller du Toit Cloete/University of Western Cape South African family law conference in Cape Town. I have now spoken at that conference in 2016, 2018, 2020, and virtually in 2021.*

In 2015 I received an award for service from the LGBTI Legal Service. I had been instrumental in rounding up family lawyers to get the service started. I had celebrated being one of the volunteers on the first night with pink champagne and pink cake. I also had the honour, along with the Honourable Michael Kirby, of speaking at the 6th anniversary celebrations of that service, held in Brisbane's Supreme Court.

In 2015 I was recognised in a ceremony at Brisbane's City Hall as the LGBTIQ+ Advocate of the Year.

*My husband Mitchell and me the night I was humbled to receive the LGBTIQ+ Advocate of the Year Award.*

My husband Mitchell and I led the Pride march in Brisbane that year, which was an extraordinary honour.

Mitchell and I were co-founders of Pride in Law, and I spoke at its opening- in the Supreme Court in Brisbane.

In 2020 I received the inaugural Pride in Law Award, after which the Queensland Law Society called me *"leading Queensland and internationally renowned surrogacy solicitor"*[35]. The judging panel included the Presidents of the Queensland Law Society and the Bar Association of Queensland.

My experience in this field is unparalleled in Australia. I am recognised internationally as an expert. I have given expert evidence on a number of occasions concerning surrogacy, including in two cases in the UK – one concerning Australian surrogacy[36] law and the other in 2021 concerning Cambodian surrogacy law.

In 2014 I was interviewed by the world's media as an expert concerning the terrible *Baby Gammy* case in Thailand[37] [38]. Mr and Mrs Farnell lived in Bunbury, Western Australia and underwent surrogacy in Thailand. On the face of it, this was unlawful in Western Australia to do so. Mr Farnell was a convicted pedophile. The surrogate, Mrs Chanbua wasn't told. Mrs Chanbua, from Thailand, put her age up improperly. She didn't tell the Farnell's.

Two embryos were implanted by the doctor, Dr Pisit. Good practice in surrogacy is usually to implant one, as having twins increases risks to the babies and to the surrogate. The two children born were subsequently known as Gammy (a boy) and Pypah (a girl). Gammy was identified in utero as having Down syndrome. It turns out he also had a congenital heart defect. When born, he was kept by Ms Chanbua. As it turns out, this was because she wanted to keep him, not because the Farnell's didn't want him. They desperately wanted him. In the pre-coup environment in Bangkok, it was unsafe for them to stay, so they returned hastily to Western Australia. They subsequently started court proceedings.

The matter spilled out into the world's media in August 2014, resulting in a media firestorm, including a pack of media permanently camped outside the Farnell's' home. Every aspect of the story seemed more lurid than the last. The Thai Government immediately cracked down on foreigners undertaking surrogacy. Australian intended parents and their surrogates who were halfway through journeys were trapped. I was contacted by seemingly every media organisation on the planet, including the *New York Times* and *Wall Street Journal* and *Dolly* (an Australian teen girls' magazine).

I have often spoken in the media about surrogacy and ART issues, for example giving Joe Donor a serve on 60 Minutes Australia. He was an American who flew here to be a sperm donor by sex or donation- and had "fathered" 100 children so far, but had annual health checks[39].

In 2018, UK family lawyer extraordinaire and friend, the late Anne-Marie Hutchinson OBE, QC (Hon) and I devised bringing experts together from around the world for the first time to discuss surrogacy- what the research told us, how surrogacy was regulated differently around the world, and what the future held. Ultimately our idea morphed into the International Surrogacy Forum, with about 200 attendees[40]. The Forum was a spectacular success. It helped persuade the then UN Special Rapporteur for the sale and sexual exploitation of children not to seek to ban all international surrogacy.

The Forum[41] was held in 2019 at the University of Cambridge and co-sponsored by the University, the International Academy of Family Lawyers and the American Bar Association. As it turns out, I was the only organisor who could not go- as the timing of the conference was just before my daughter Elizabeth was due.

I am the founder and director of the LGBT Family Law Institute in Australia, part of a worldwide movement centred on the LGBT Family Law Institute in the US[42] (which in turn is a joint venture of the LGBT Bar Association and the National Center for Lesbian Rights), and the oldest group in Australia of lawyers advocating for LGBTIQ people. I was deeply honoured when Bill Singer[43] from New Jersey, who had founded the LGBT Family Law Institute in the US, asked me if I could set up a group in Australia. He did so when I was attending the first meeting of the UK and Ireland LGBT Family Law Institute, run by another surrogacy lawyer, Natalie Gamble[44].

I am a director of Access Australia's Infertility Network Limited[45], and a director of the Fertility Society of Australia and New Zealand[46].

In addition to acting for intended parents, surrogates and donors, I have for many years been an independent children's lawyer on the panel maintained by Legal Aid Queensland and I bring a child's rights focus to my work. I have been fortunate to be appointed as independent children's lawyer in cases involving ART.

One of those was a case in regional Queensland of a traditional surrogacy where the surrogate lied to the intended fathers- as she was already pregnant to someone else, and then tried to pass the child off to another couple and to a single woman. None of the parties had counselling or legal advice. The intended father (who had been the would be surrogate's friend) was crushed. She after all had lied to him by not letting him know she was already pregnant (when she well knew) before he gave her sperm at her house. She then in effect blackmailed the intended fathers to proceed with the surrogacy (this being her plan all along.) She had then terminated the surrogacy two weeks before the child was born on an entirely unreasonable basis- because his sister (who had been the "surrogate's" friend) would have involvement with the child as the child's aunt. This was a clear case of why there are safeguards under the legislation to have counselling and legal advice before entering into surrogacy arrangements, so that trainwreck cases like this can be avoided.

I have advised a number of IVF clinics, sperm banks and would-be egg and embryo banks concerning ART regulation in different parts of Australia.

Every day to me is a blessing. I am honoured to help others achieve the dream of parenthood. I am reminded of the words of the human swan, Sacha Dench[47]:

> *"There's no point feeling doom and gloom because that doesn't get you anywhere, the only thing that gets you anywhere is focusing on the solutions."*

[1] See: https://en.wikipedia.org/wiki/Baby_M.

[2] In a case litigated 10 years later: Re Evelyn [1998] FamCA 55 www8.austlii.edu.au/cgi-bin/viewdoc/au/cases/cth/FamCA/1998/55.html that's exactly what happened. The child went to live with the traditional surrogate and her husband.

[3] Sociologist Sujay Kentlyn many years ago described these letters or the then version of them as "alphabet soup", which continues to evolve. I apologise for anyone who is left out. It is inadvertent on my part.

[4] Because of the effect of the then Surrogate Parenthood Act 1988 (Qld).

[5] And I have had clients move to where they can undertake surrogacy lawfully. The problems exist now. When I recently had clients say: "Couldn't we just pretend that we are there, in the house we own, across the border?"; I responded with: "So aside from the criminal issues under the surrogacy legislation, you want to also commit a much more serious offence, such as attempting to pervert the course of justice? [pause] Are you NUTS?" They got the point.

[6] https://www.smh.com.au/national/and-baby-makes-five-the-senator-his-wife-and-the-surrogate-mothers-20061107-gdort7.html.

[7] And other comments by Lawrence Springborg about gays can be seen here: https://www.starobserver.com.au/news/national-news/queensland-news/past-homophobic-comments-re-emerge-to-haunt-queensland-lnp-leader-and-mp/132286

[8] Which can be found here, at 112B: https://www.americanbar.org/content/dam/aba/administrative/house_of_delegates/2016_hod_midyear_meeting_electronic_report_book.authcheckdam.pdf.

[9] https://www.modern-family-law.com/about.html

[10] https://www.iarcsurrogacy.com/about-iarc/

[11] https://www.iflg.net/who-we-are/rich-vaughn-esq/

[12] https://www.circlesurrogacy.com/about/meet-circle/dean-hutchison-esq

[13] https://www.hcch.net/en/home

[14] For example, the 1980 Hague Convention on Civil Aspects of International Child Abduction.

[15] Indeed the International Convention on the Rights of the Child recognises that children have a right to an identity.

[16] About the different laws in Australia about surrogacy and bringing a baby back to Australia who had been born to intended parents in the US. I was jealous of colleagues who were speaking, for example, from Italy, where they only had one system of law. I had to cover nine systems of law: each State and Territory and the Commonwealth.

[17] LWV v LMH [2012] QChC 26: https://archive.sclqld.org.au/qjudgment/2012/QChC12-026.pdf.

27

18. And I am thankful to my colleague Amy Sanders-Robbins who asked me if I was available to act for the surrogate in such an important case. She knew I had prepared submissions in another case on the same lines, but the other case had not yet been heard.

19. I had, for example, when he was Brisbane's Lord Mayor, invited him to speak at the then Brisbane Gay and Lesbian Business Network. He came and spoke, the first LNP member to do so.

20. By 2015, Mr Bleijie had changed his mind and supported gay and lesbian couples marrying and entering into civil partnerships: https://pageprovan.com.au/bleijie-supports-gay-marriage/.

21. For reasons unknown, Missouri, New Mexico and South Dakota were excluded.

22. Re Grosvenor [2017] FamCA 366 http://www.austlii.edu.au/cgi-bin/viewdoc/au/cases/cth/FamCA/2017/366.html ; Sigley and Sigley [2018] FamCA 3 http://www.austlii.edu.au/cgi-bin/viewdoc/au/cases/cth/FamCA/2018/3.html ; Rose [2018] FamCA 978 http://www.austlii.edu.au/cgi-bin/viewdoc/au/cases/cth/FamCA/2018/978.html ; Allan and Peters [2018] FamCA 1063http://www.austlii.edu.au/cgi-bin/viewdoc/au/cases/cth/FamCA/2018/1063.html.

23. Re Halvard [2016] FamCA 1051 http://www.austlii.edu.au/cgi-bin/viewdoc/au/cases/cth/FamCA/2016/1051.html.

24. Bernieres & Dhopal [2017] FamCAFC 180 http://www.austlii.edu.au/cgi-bin/viewdoc/au/cases/cth/FamCAFC/2017/180.html.

25. Article 3, though to be fair to the court, although Australia has signed up to the Convention, it is not part of our domestic law. Nevertheless the Family Law Act includes the Convention when considering matters to do with parenting: section 60B(4) (4): "An additional object of this Part is to give effect to the Convention on the Rights of the Child done at New York on 20 November 1989", and the High Court said in Teoh's case [1995] HCA 20 that parents and children had a legitimate expectation in the absence of statute or regulation to the contrary that the decision maker will take the Convention into account when making decisions about children. The Court in Bernieres did not mention the Convention.

26. Article 8.

27. Masson v Parsons [2019] HCA 21 http://www.austlii.edu.au/cgi-bin/viewdoc/au/cases/cth/HCA//2019/21.html.

28. https://www.united.com/ual/en/us/fly/contact/reservations/australia.html

29. https://www.yourtravelexpert.com.au/

30. https://www.growingfamilies.org/

31. https://www.facebook.com/farandwidemigration/

32. See my article for Bionews: https://www.bionews.org.uk/page_95560.

33. Section 16: (1) "A surrogate mother has the same rights to manage her pregnancy and birth as any other pregnant woman. (2) A provision of a lawful surrogacy agreement that

is inconsistent with subsection (1), or that purports to require the consent of the intended parents in relation to the management of the surrogate mother's pregnancy, the health of the unborn child to which the lawful surrogacy agreement relates, or the birth of a child to which the lawful surrogacy agreement relates, is void and of no effect. (3) This section applies despite any provision of a lawful surrogacy agreement to the contrary." I am also delighted that following representations I and others made that section 44A has been inserted into the Assisted Reproductive Treatment Act 2008 (Vic) to the same effect.

[34] Section 7(1)(a): "the human rights of all parties to a lawful surrogacy agreement, including any child born as a result of the agreement, must be respected".

[35] https://www.qlsproctor.com.au/2020/11/surrogacy-law-leader-named-inaugural-pride-in-law-award-recipient/

[36] In the matter of Z (A Child) (No 2) [2016] EWFC 119 http://www.bailii.org/ew/cases/EWHC/Fam/2016/1191.html.

[37] For example: https://www.dailymail.co.uk/news/article-2717364/Australian-parents-Gammy-met-Chinese-mail-order-bride-agency.html, https://www.news.com.au/lifestyle/parenting/babies/lawyer-stephen-page-says-thai-surrogacy-baby-gammy-case-preventable/news-story/76a53c793ab0f13cc4be2f02c824d469, https://www.abc.net.au/news/2014-08-12/advocates-call-for-commercial-surrogacy-to-be-legalised/5666206, https://www.smh.com.au/national/gammy-who-is-telling-the-truth-20140805-3d6n1.html, https://www.sbs.com.au/news/sites/sbs.com.au.news/files/transcripts/363753_insight_surrogacy_transcript.html, https://www.theguardian.com/australia-news/2014/oct/09/surrogate-baby-left-in-india-by-australian-couple-was-not-trafficked-investigation-finds.

[38] And then the media wanted to talk about surrogacy regulation more broadly, such as when I described Australian surrogacy laws in 2014 on AM with Chris Uhlmann to be an "absolute mess": https://www.abc.net.au/am/content/2014/s4103294.htmh. Although there have been some changes, significant challenges remain for those wanting to do surrogacy across Australian state borders.

[39] https://www.youtube.com/watch?v=NGhbcTGZmkI.

[40] See for example the story of the Mennesson family from France: https://www.youtube.com/watch?v=36-5WW0AICY.

[41] See: https://lgbtqbar.org/programs/member-practice-area-groups/family-law-institute/.

[42] https://lgbtqbar.org/programs/member-practice-area-groups/family-law-institute/

[43] https://www.singerfedun.com/bill-singer.html

[44] https://www.ngalaw.co.uk/.

[45] https://hub.givar.com/cause/55f8f3fb303c421100fa8d10.

[46] https://www.fertilitysociety.com.au/about/#board

[47] For more about Sacha Dench: https://www.sachadench.com/

CHAPTER 2

# ABOUT ME – MY PERSONAL JOURNEY

I have had three children. This was not part of any grand plan on my part- but it has been my life's journey.

## Experiencing infertility

When I left university, my goals in life were pretty simple. I wanted to get a job as a lawyer, maybe go into politics (which I decided very quickly was not for me), get married and have kids. What I didn't expect and could not possibly have imagined, was that I would have several marriages later, that I am now married to a man, that I would be a leader in my field in fertility law and have three children, including becoming a dad through surrogacy.

When I fought tenaciously in 2012/2013 to protect Queenslanders' rights to become parents through surrogacy (**see chapter 1**), I did not imagine in my wildest dreams that it would ever impact on me.

After I got married the first time my then wife[48] and I went to her gynaecologist. My wife had endometriosis. The doctor, a gruff old man, said:

*"The only cure is to get pregnant".*

We sat with our jaws agape. I said:

> *"Well, we're broke and in our early 20s. We want to be like everyone else – have a house and then have children".*

His response:

> *"What am I, a financial planner? I'm a doctor".*

Shocked by his virtual slap across the chops, we started trying, living by the book. Nothing worked. One day, my wife said to me:

> *"Maybe you've got a problem too. You should get your sperm checked."*

She was quite sensible about it. I wasn't. I responded with male hubris and finger-pointing:

> *"I haven't got a problem. You've got endometriosis. I've got 100% Aussie super gold sperm."*

I'm embarrassed that I said those words, but nevertheless, I did. She said:

> *"How do you know until you've been tested?"*

I said, firmly:

> *"Because I know!".*

I was an idiot. Of course, I didn't know. Nevertheless, I refused to get tested. It took about another three months of trying before I agreed to get tested. When I provided my sperm, I was shocked. I had low motility – slow swimmers. This didn't mean that we couldn't get there – it just lowered the chances. I suddenly realised that it wasn't just her problem and that science would cure everything. The doctor had told us that there was only a 24% chance of success through IVF if conceiving naturally didn't work – but I took that 24% to mean 100%. I had all confidence in the scientific certainty of IVF. It is funny that all those years later I can still remember that percentage of 24%. Now my world had been turned upside down. No longer was it my wife's problem, but it became *my* problem. I suddenly thought it's *not when* I would become a dad (something that

I'd always dreamed of since about the ages of 4 or 5), *but if* I became a dad.

I worked in Logan, which was a poorer part of Brisbane. I had clients from throughout Logan. Many of the people I saw were incredibly fertile and some of them should not have had children. I looked around the local area and thought:

> *"How come **they** can have children and **I** can't?"*

I'm asthmatic. About twice a year I have a major asthma attack. There is nothing as scary as no matter how many times you move your lungs, no air gets in. At that moment I fear that I will die. I think to myself:

> *"God, why have you punished me so? How come everyone else can move their chest and lungs and can breathe and I can't?"*

The worst occasion was when I was 17 and through the quick actions of my future wife, my life was saved by a doctor coming and injecting me when my lips had turned blue.

> *I had the same reaction about not becoming a father. I started to look up at the ceilings and I'd look at a cornice - in particular into the corner of the cornice - and say to myself:*

There was no logic to this. But it was my reality.

I knew from the age of 4 or 5 that I was to be a father. Now my reality seemed to be otherwise. It was profoundly depressing.

My then wife and I had classic infertility. We kept persisting. We got lucky. I was blessed with two sons. By sheer luck we didn't have to do IVF.

While my journey to parenthood is different from everyone else's, I have stared into the abyss and despaired as to whether I would ever become a father. It is an awful place to be. I have called this book *When not if* because that is the reality of surrogacy- sooner or later you will get there. This is a story of hope, based on reality, not on spin.

## Mitchell appears

In 2013 I met my husband to be, Mitchell. It was love at first sight. We were absolutely besotted with each other, and still are. I came out.

We weren't allowed to get married in Australia at that stage. We didn't want to wait another second. In 2015 I had to go to the United States to speak at conferences in San Francisco and Chicago. The trip was to last just over a week. We were going to spend a couple of days in Vegas on the way back, staying with friends, one of whom worked at an IVF clinic there. Three weeks out, Mitchell said:

> *"Why don't we get married there?"*

And so we did. My best man was Dr Said Daneshmand, who is now at San Diego Fertility Center[49]. We were blessed to have a small group of American friends attend on minimal notice. At a time that we were denied the ability to be married in Australia, it was comforting to know that the United States welcomed us as husbands.

## Making a family

Of course, marriage wasn't the end of our journey together, but merely the beginning. Mitchell told me that he wanted to become a dad. I was immediately opposed to becoming a dad again. I had been there, done that. I'm older than Mitchell. I thought I would never stop working. After a very short while, I realised that I was stupid and selfish. I was imposing on Mitchell the same that might have been once imposed on me – that he would never ever become a dad. I came to my senses.

We decided that we wanted to become parents together. And then something magical happened. A woman close to us, I'll call her Roxanne, was visiting our house one day and said:

> *"I love both of you. I've had all my own children. I don't want to have any more. My uterus isn't being used. I want to be your surrogate."*

We both cried tears of joy. I was overwhelmed by this extraordinary generosity of spirit. It was one of the most amazing moments of my life. At the same time, I had another emotion going in my head:

*"This is what my clients go through."*

Another woman close to us, I'll call her Jen, offered to be our egg donor. Again, I was amazed at this generosity of spirit. It was one thing to have clients undergo this journey, and for me to look on, and yet another for me to go through this journey that was tied up in who we were, our love for each other, our marriage, our planned family and future lives together.

We were very lucky. Most intended parents who set out on the surrogacy journey aren't able to have someone they know as their surrogate and someone they know as their egg donor. Only 1 in 5 surrogacy journeys for Australian intended parents occur in Australia. Four fifths occur overseas – **see chapter 10- Numbers don't lie, Going overseas or Domestic** and even worse in WA - **see chapter 27**. Our journey involved people we knew and loved- and all occurring locally.

We got underway. Our journey was not an easy one – and was one of the more difficult that I've ever seen. We had medical issues with our surrogate and egg donor that had to be sorted.

They were.

We went through all the usual steps, of course:

- All the medical checks
- Counselling with our egg donor Jen. We were amazed at her generosity in donating her genetic material, having daily injections of hormones in her stomach to enable her to donate and then being prepared to undertake the risks of egg collection[50].
- Counselling with our surrogate Roxanne. I remain in thrall of Roxanne for willingly and generously becoming pregnant and giving birth and taking the risk of death to enable Mitch and me to start a family. In Queensland there is counselling before entering onto the surrogacy arrangement and then after the birth a different counsellor has to undertake an assessment - to make sure that the making of a parentage order is in the child's best

interests. The first counsellor I approached declined to do so after obtaining ethical advice:

> *"You must understand Stephen that as a friend of yours, the specific ethical advice I have received means I cannot help."*

- Legal advice. This got a bit tricky. While I could advise Mitch, the conflict of interest was obvious. I could not advise myself. We were required to get legal advice from someone else. Thankfully my then associate Karen Gough agreed to give advice. When it came time to sit down and go through the advice, Karen said:

    > *"There's no point giving you advice as you're the expert, Stephen."*

I replied:

> *"Can you please do it, Karen? If both Mitch and I don't get the advice, and we don't appear to understand the advice given, then the surrogacy arrangement is non-compliant, a parentage order can't be made and we won't be recognized as the parents."*

I am thankful that Karen then gave the advice.

We had financial issues which slowed everything down. Things were tight. The IVF clinic changed its policy, so we found that the cost of IVF with that clinic jumped. We changed clinics. This had to be handled delicately, because I worked closely with the first clinic.

### The longest nanosecond

When we had each of our three implantations they had to be paid for by us. Each cost $3,000. As soon as the implantation was over, we walked out the front of the clinic. The lovely woman behind the desk looked at me and said, each time:

*"That'll be $3,000, Mr Page."*

My brain then went through this dance, all in a nanosecond:

*"Oh my God. That is a huge amount of money. That will take forever to pay."*

Then:

*"Have I got it on the card?"*

Realising I could pay straightaway on the card, but usually using it with PayWave:

*"What's my pin number again?"*

I then turned to the woman behind the counter, smiled and put in my pin number.

## Why won't the taxpayer fund Medicare for surrogacy?

I get asked this question by clients a lot.

Undertaking surrogacy, however you do it, is not cheap. The federal Government will not give Medicare for surrogacy work: **see chapter 6**. Of the about $250 million[51] the Government spends on Medicare for IVF and related services each year, it refuses to spend 0.3% extra at just under $900,000 a year to provide Medicare rebates for surrogacy.

The only obvious answer about why the federal government will not fund surrogacy is because of the perception that there would be a backlash by helping gay people become parentzs. The Australian Christian Lobby, for example, is opposed to ALL surrogacy, no matter whether it is commercial or altruistic, traditional or gestational: the lot, even between sisters. The Australian Christian Lobby said this in its submission to the House of Representatives Surrogacy Inquiry (2016)[52]:

*"ACL is opposed to the legalisation of surrogacy, in any form, whether altruistic or commercial. ACL explains in this submission that the practice of surrogacy is inherently unjust to children and exploitative of the surrogate mother. ACL makes 3 recommendations reflecting this position, including the prohibition of surrogacy domestically and internationally for Australian citizens and the resourcing of law enforcement to ensure a deterrent to the practice."*

The cost to the taxpayer of an IVF cycle (what is commonly called a round of IVF) was estimated in 2015 to be about $5,000[53]. When I calculated the numbers by using the 2021 Medicare rebate, I came up with $4,635.05. Canstar Research in 2019 estimated the cost of one round of IVF to be over $8,000[54]. The out of pocket cost estimated by Canstar was $3,380 on average, leaving the Medicare portion at $4,620, or pretty well on zthe money for my calculations.

The best estimate for the number of IVF cycles undertaken in the most recent year reported (2019) is 188[55]. The pregnancy rate is 40% and about one third of the cycles end up in a live birth. The number of gestational carrier cycles is 225 across Australia and New Zealand. If the number of IVF cycles for gestational surrogacy is undertaken at the same rate in Australia and New Zealand (something we don't know), then with New Zealand having a population of 5 million and Australia at 25 million, that 225 reduces down to 188 for the number in Australia.

Based on that cost per IVF cycle of $4,635.05, the likely cost to the taxpayer would be:

$4,635.05 cost per IVF cycle to the taxpayer x 188 IVF cycles = $871,389.40.

By comparison:

- The Commonwealth government decided to spend $660 million on a commuter car park scheme[56], or 757 times as much.
- It costs the taxpayer $350,000 to hold a singzle refugee on Nauru *per month*[57]. The cost of holding that one refugee for three months will cost more than the cost of subsiding medical treatment for surrogacy through Medicare.
- Like them or loathe them, each federal politician costs the taxpayer about $1 million a year[58].
- When the federal government decided to intervene in three High Court cases concerning the closing of state borders due to Covid-19, the total cost was $1 million, part of which was described as "a stupendous waste of money".

Our journey ultimately took over four years. At one point I thought:

> *"Why's this happening to me? How come all my clients or most of my clients can have children well and truly before we do? I do more surrogacy than anyone. One would think that my journey would be quick."*

It was the same kind of negative thinking I had when having asthma attacks and when I had previously struggled to become a dad.

After a split second came my response:

> *"You idiot. You can't control this process, much as you can't control the behaviour of other drivers on the road, although you want to."*

My philosophy in life is that I want to get in and get out as quickly as I can. I have the same philosophy when helping clients. I want my clients' journey to be as quick, cheap and above all as stress free as possible. In summary, my views are:

> *"Oh Lord, give me patience. But give it to me quick!"*

## The first pregnancy: miscarriage

Roxanne became pregnant on the first attempt. Eight weeks later she had a miscarriage. We were devastated. The doctor told us that the almost certain reason it'd happened wasn't because of our surrogate. Having seen it before, I did not doubt the doctor.

Nevertheless, Roxanne felt guilty that she hadn't provided us with a child (the typical reaction of a surrogate in those circumstances).

When the doctor told us that, we were determined to have another go, but I couldn't help wondering:

> *"If our DNA is the problem then what about the next one? It's going to be the same DNA."*

## The second pregnancy: ectopic

The next attempt was also successful. Roxanne got pregnant. Then something seemed to go wrong. Roxanne had a bleed and it seemed the baby was not thriving. The three of us went to see the doctor on a Friday. He told us it may be an ectopic pregnancy – where the embryo ends up stuck in the fallopian tube and if not removed immediately can rupture, causing the potential death of the woman. He said to run some tests, but in the meantime assume it is ectopic, just in case. If ectopic, immediate surgery was required. Until January 2021, I had never seen an ectopic pregnancy with surrogacy in my practice- but it was happening in our journey.

We agreed that tests needed to be done and that Roxanne and I would again see the doctor on Monday. Mitchell couldn't come due to work. On the Monday, our worst fears were realised. We were told that it was an ectopic pregnancy and that immediate surgery was needed. That happened within a few hours. I stayed with Roxanne. I said:

> *"I love you. We didn't set out on this journey to hurt anyone else. Whether Mitch or I have a baby is beside the point. I couldn't live with myself if something bad happened to you."*

We cried and hugged. Surgery went well.

## The third pregnancy: success!

Some months later after she recovered, we had another go. Our surrogate became pregnant a third time. Everything worked – save that our daughter Elizabeth almost died in childbirth. Of my three children, my first and last almost died in childbirth. In each case it was a reminder to me of the benefits of good hospital care. Both survived!

After several days in hospital, Roxanne had been induced at 9 a.m. Elizabeth was not engaging properly, which triggered the induction. By 5 p.m. not much was happening. Mitch decided to go home and feed the cats. He came back at 7 p.m. and not much was happening at that point. He missed the big drama. In addition to the drugs to induce (which increased Roxanne's and therefore Elizabeth's pulse, blood pressure and temperature), Roxanne had been given an epidural. This would have counteracted these effects.

What we didn't know was that the epidural hadn't worked. It hadn't gone into the spinal cavity. Roxanne's pulse, blood pressure and temperature were all significantly up. So was our baby's. Elizabeth was being cooked in front of me. When Roxanne was evidently in great pain, the midwife came in. The vital signs were very concerning, particularly for Elizabeth. I was doing everything I could to calm Roxanne (who was starting to panic, because of the effect on her body), and to cool her, by applying cool towels, one after another. In the midst of this drama, when I am seeing the pulse blood pressure and temperature of our baby going up and up, he midwife looked at those monitors and said:

*"Don't die on me darling."*

She was talking about our baby. I did not react. I thought that to react at that moment could have jeopardized both Elizabeth's and Roxanne's health. I stayed calm. Luckily things were brought under control. An anaesthetist came in and performed a second epidural. It worked!

By the time Mitch came back, Roxanne was sleeping, exhausted. I was sprawled in a recliner chair nearby in the semi-darkness, barely able to stay awake.

It took a few hours more for Elizabeth to be born. She got stuck coming out. A doctor came in and assisted. Elizabeth was born after his actions, in the early hours of the morning. I cut the chord. Mitch held her first, then I did and then our surrogate did. We were all exhausted. We all cried tears of joy at this miracle before us.

All the usual tests had then to be run by the hospital.

In the generation between when my sons were born and when Elizabeth was born, there have been dramatic changes in maternity hospitals. Back then, there was the latest technology in the birthing suite- and two midwives for the whole experience, an obstetrician or anaesthetist moving in and out as required.

These days, it is quite a different experience. The first obvious difference was that there was only one midwife in the room, occasionally supplemented by another- and an obstetrician or anesthetist moving in and out as required. Roxanne had chosen to give birth as a public patient, as opposed to a private patient which is how both my sons had been born. While we were happy for her to be private patient, she had decided to give birth that way- which of course was her choice.

> ### Bodily autonomy
>
> Surrogates, like any other woman, should have bodily autonomy over the pregnancy and birth- and I am glad that South Australia, Tasmania and Victoria have copied in their *Surrogacy Acts* this statement from the Queensland *Surrogacy Act 2010* (Qld)[59]:
>
> > *"A birth mother has the same rights to manage her pregnancy and birth as any other* pregnant woman."
>
> While judge made law, our common law, says that too, it is a much more powerful statement to see that Parliament has upheld this right in legislation. Whether it is a surrogacy arrangement in those states or elsewhere, I am always keen to ensure that it is said in black and white in the surrogacy arrangement that the surrogate has bodily autonomy over her pregnancy and childbirth. When I discuss it with my clients who are surrogates, all express the wish to have the express clause in black and white in the agreement that they have control over their bodies.
>
> I have consistently urged that this right to bodily autonomy be clearly stated in legislation. I have made representations, it would appear successfully from the results, to have the law changed in South Australia and Victoria, so that this bodily autonomy is part of the legal landscape with surrogacy.
>
> But I digress.

Aside from the cost difference and that we did not have a choice of specialist, there was little difference in the quality of expertise that was given to assist in the birth, or the accommodation provided afterwards.

Just over four hours after Elizabeth was born, we were cleared to take Elizabeth back to her room. After almost 24 hours of being in the birthing room, we were exhausted. Our little entourage of four and our midwife, with Elizabeth in her special wheeled crib, snaked our way back upstairs for somewhere to crash.

Then we experienced three quirks of hospital.

## The first quirk

Mitch and I got a room. Elizabeth was able to be in the same room as Mitch and me. Roxanne was next door. Our hospital, a large maternity hospital, had a surrogacy policy, one of the first in the country, and a surrogacy co-ordinator. They made sure, if possible, for Roxanne and us to have separate rooms and for Elizabeth to be in the same room as Mitch and me. Nevertheless, when the three of us had turned up to antenatal class, the lesson seemed directed at straight couples. That experience had seemed a little odd, because every time we turned up to hospital for a scan or a check up, we were warmly welcomed.

Not everyone gets a separate room. Not every baby gets to spend time with its parents immediately after birth. Maternity hospitals are busy, crazy places where babies come all at once, or not at all. Having a separate room depends on how many babies are being born at the time.

## Don't bet you'll get separate rooms

As late as 2018, a hospital in regional Queensland refused to allow the intended mum in what the hospital was told was a surrogacy journey to stay in the hospital. This was a small part of the **story at the end of chapter 1**.

In 2012 I was acting for a surrogate and her husband. The regional Queensland hospital (a different one to that in 2018) refused to allow the intended mother to stay in the hospital as the mother. I tried to get the then head of maternity to see sense, without luck. She told me, firmly:

*"The woman who gives birth is the mother. The intended mother can come during visiting hours only. At our hospital we don't discriminate. We are very busy. We have only so many beds and rooms. We are packed full all the time. We don't have enough beds and rooms. [She said it again, for emphasis.] The child will stay with the mother. The intended mother can come and spend time with the child during visiting hours, and be taught to feed, bathe and change the baby- but she can't stay. We have no resources."*

This was part of the lecture I received from the head of maternity for my temerity for suggesting that the baby be with the intended mum from birth- and for the potential damage to the child if that didn't happen. I had been asked by the solicitor for the intended parents if I, as solicitor for the surrogate and her husband, could get the head of maternity to see sense- because the intended parents and their solicitor had had no luck.

I, too, had no luck.

I tried to suggest to my client to give birth somewhere else. There was nowhere else.

When my client came to give birth, the midwives were enraptured by her generosity of being a surrogate for someone else. They had never experienced surrogacy before. Lo and behold! A room was found for the intended mum, and the baby stayed with her (not my client) in hospital. The midwives could see the reality, even if the head of maternity couldn't. The intended mum and baby were discharged before my client was. Everyone was very happy once that obstruction had been overcome. To channel Attenborough again:

> *"So animals and ourselves, to continue the line, will endure all kinds of hardship, overcome all kinds of difficulties, and eventually the next generation appears."*

In our exhaustion, we felt so lucky to have a separate room, with our daughter in there with us, fast asleep. It was beautiful. The room had two beds, or more precisely, a bed and a hard uncomfortable thing that seemed to be a couch attached to the wall. I said to Mitch:

*"You take the bed, I'll take the couch."*

Mitch said:

*"You take the bed, I'll take the couch."*

I prevailed. Mitch is shorter than me. If I took the bed or the couch, my feet would hang over the end. Hospitals being hospitals, an extension to the bed could be found, but it would take hours to arrive. I figured he at least could have some sleep while I slept with my feet dangling over the end of the couch.

We crashed. Did I say we were exhausted? I fell asleep instantly, the three of us in our own little place of heaven together for the first time as a family. In the midst of the fog of exhaustion, life was beautiful. Our journey surrogacy journey had almost been completed- but our journey as a family had begun.

That blissful sleep lasted 20 minutes, before the first nurse came in, requiring paperwork for this, that or the other.

## The second quirk

Hungry, I then discovered the second quirk of the hospital. The hospital had innovated with a menu. Having been to many hospitals over the years, I had no grand expectations of hospital food, which has always seemed an oxymoron to me. But this hospital had a menu! And room service! One could order a meal- and it would be delivered right to the bed. Hooray! All I wanted was breakfast (as did Roxanne and Mitch). Roxanne had been in the hospital for a few days, and had praised the room service, though after a few days the meals tended to become the same choice.

Most people who go to maternity hospital as patients of course go as singles or couples- not a trio. The menu was devised about having a patient and their support person, for example the woman's partner. Not a third person.

While Roxanne and Mitch could and did immediately order brekkie, I couldn't. I was the odd one out. When I sought to order, I discovered that I was *"not authorised"* to order meals. This was not something mentioned anywhere by the hospital, and something new to discover in the morning while sleep deprived. I then had to get to the lift, go downstairs into the bowels of the hospital and then order and pay for some vouchers. Then I had to go back to the ward and speak to the nurse in charge to make sure my vouchers were validated. Then, about 40 minutes later after talking to the nurse, I was able to order. And then eventually, breakfast appeared- a beautiful hot breakfast, my first breakfast as a dad to Elizabeth. Bliss!

*Mitch and I in our room at the hospital with Elizabeth. The pic does not begin to describe our bliss or exhaustion.*

And of course the hospital did all the right things about our care for Elizabeth- checking her vital signs, doing the basics with us about feeding, bathing and changing her, looking after our surrogate to make sure she was OK, and providing formula.

Anyone who has been to any form of hospital knows the drill: just when you think it is time to sleep, someone knocks on the door or just barges in anyway to do something- a nurse checking for vital signs, a doctor doing the rounds, someone checking that we had breakfast (*"Yes he did, but I am still waiting, thank you very much for asking"*), someone to bring meals, and take them away, the cleaner, and on and on.

We were thankful that Roxanne had agreed to provide colostrum straight after the birth, vital for our daughter's immunity. The amount of colostrum is tiny, smaller than the fingernail on my pinky- but filled with protections for her later in life. Roxanne also agreed to provide breastmilk- not to breast feed- but as often happens after birth, it took a while for her body to kick in. We had agreed that she would not breastfeed. In Roxanne's words:

> *"The two of you are the parents. I'm not. For me to breastfeed would be icky."*

Formula was essential to a hungry baby. We were fortunate that for months later Roxanne continued to give us frozen breast milk. Most intended parents are not so lucky. In the course of providing that breast milk, nature's beautiful process meant that Roxanne was helping repair her body, as well as providing vital food and protection to Elizabeth[60].

## The third quirk

Another change between when my sons were born and now, is that the time for women to be discharged from hospital has been compressed. Women who have given birth are usually discharged the same day. However, the law still considers the surrogate to be mum. This means (unlike the regional Queensland experience above) that the child is never discharged before the surrogate. In reality, everyone walks out the front at once, the intended parents with the baby to their car and the surrogate to hers.

If only we had automatic recognition of the intended parents at birth (except of course in the rare disputed cases where a judge can decide) then the baby can go home when its needs demand it, and the surrogate can go home when her needs demand it. Automatic recognition is common in the US, and has recently been suggested for the UK[61]- because surrogates don't see themselves as the mothers. They see the intended parents as the parents- and that the surrogates are giving the gift of life to the intended parents for their child. Typically, surrogates don't want another child- and especially don't want someone else's child- one that is not genetically theirs.

After what seemed the longest day ever, news came late that afternoon that Roxanne was well enough to go home, and that she was being discharged. Then the S word was mentioned: **surrogacy**. Roxanne, having spent a few days in hospital away from family, was desperate to go home. The problem was that checks had to be run on Elizabeth. Elizabeth had to stay overnight. Roxanne, the woman who gave birth was being discharged before the baby. Despite this hospital being extraordinarily busy, and having had experience with surrogacy for about 10 years[62], it had never come across this scenario- the birth mother going home first.

What happened next was awful. The decision making went through the hospital chain of command:

- a midwife
- then a second midwife
- then a third midwife
- then a hospital executive
- then a second hospital executive
- then a third hospital executive
- and finally, the hospital lawyer.

Roxanne and I were in the corridor when a hospital executive told us that in the eyes of the lawyer, Roxanne, as a single woman who had just given birth, was the only parent, and that it was "*advisable*" that she not go home now and leave the baby in the hospital. Despite my role as a specialist in this field and one of Elizabeth's two dads, my protests were in vain. I may as well have been talking to the walls.

Without discussing at the time, Roxanne and I knew instantly was "advisable" meant. It meant that as the sole parent, if Roxanne abandoned the child in hospital by going home, the Department of Child Safety would be involved, with all that entailed.

We were gutted. Roxanne immediately burst into tears:

*"I just want to go home."*

She then went to her room, alone, and bawled for a long time. When each of Mitch and I checked on her, Roxanne said:

*"I just want to be alone."*

She was completely powerless. It was though she had been violated. I felt completely powerless – that I could not help her in any way. It was terrible. Remembering it now as I write this is causing me to cry.

Roxanne and I were told that if Elizabeth seemed fine by the morning, she would be discharged early in the morning.

My late father had a maxim about hospitals:

*"Hospital time is not real time."*

We then discovered that maxim in practice. Due to delays from this check and that, Elizabeth (and Roxanne) was finally discharged about 4pm.

## The day after we got home

Within a day of our returning home Jen and her daughter came over. They both held Elizabeth. We all cried tears of joy. Mitch and I were so lucky.

Elizabeth will be told in due course in an age appropriate manner where she came from- **see chapter 18**.

What I didn't expect was that shortly after Elizabeth's birth, her story would be in the media, about how surrogacy is done in Australia, as opposed to how it happens in developing countries[63].

## Going to court

When it came time to obtain the court orders, I decided to appear as the lawyer for Mitch and me. For me, this was the greatest honour. Unlike most parents who let it go after the birth of their child to then apply for a parentage order, we got on with it quickly. We applied to the court within 2 months of Elizabeth's birth (which meant we had to have done the post-birth report interviews, and obtain all the affidavits in that time- see chapter…) and then waiting another month for the court date.

In making that decision, I asked Mitch at first, and then Roxanne- both of whom agreed. I then spoke to my law partner, Bruce Provan and my associate, Karen Gough, to see if either had any concerns. Neither did. I checked with my opposite number Kate Cherry who had no objection. I checked the ethical rules about acting for yourself and your partner, and came up clear. Out of an absolute abundance of caution, I checked with the Queensland Law Society. All good.

I then prepared the submissions. The first difficulty I had reflected on was whose name went on the birth certificate. Most of the time in Australia this will be the birth parent only- in our case, Roxanne. However, these was a decision in Queensland that said Mitch was also a parent (and by implication should also be shown on the birth certificate). If he were on the birth certificate, the court might be prevented from making a parentage order (as he could not be both a birth parent and an intended parent under the *Surrogacy Act 2010* (Qld)).

And if that were not awful enough, the High Court had said a month before Elizabeth was born that who was a parent under the *Family Law Act* was someone seen in the wider view of Australian society was a parent- and that it was possible that a child could have three parents[64].

At which point I decided that the right course was that the only person to be on the birth certificate was Roxanne. Neither Mitch nor I should be on it.

It's at this point I mention what I say to my clients:

*"Test cases are very interesting, except when they're your own."*

I try to avoid like the plague for my clients to have test cases. I just want them to get on with their lives- but here we were in our own test case. Who was the parent under Queensland law (and should be recognized on the birth certificate before the Court makes a parentage order, bearing in mind that if we got it wrong, there would be all the stress of an adjournment to fix the mistake)- was it:

- Roxanne alone?
- Roxanne and Mitch?
- Mitch and me?
- Mitch, Roxanne and me?

The written submissions I prepared were enormous- but they showed conclusively, I thought, that the only parent under Queensland law on the birth certificate was Roxanne.

## The morning of Court

Mitch, Elizabeth and I drove into my work in the city, a short walk away from court. Mitch and I then swore a joint affidavit as to our current circumstances, standard procedure on the morning of court of my Queensland matters. In light of the significance of the day and her involvement, Karen went with us to court.

Roxanne also came to our office. I was a bundle of nerves in going to court- the second most nervous I have been in any court appearance (The most nervous of course being in front a well known snappy judge, before I was admitted, when my barrister had double booked himself and I found myself trying to stammer out what I wanted.) Part of the reason I was nervous, of course, was because it was our matter and I had insisted on appearing as the lawyer. But I was more nervous because I did not know whether the judge would accept my submissions in what was a test case. I was sweating on getting it right.

And then there was Miss Elizabeth Page. This was not one of her best days. Many babies have walked with me the short distance to court. I have also appeared in Sydney, Melbourne and Townsville with the baby present. Some babies remain calm throughout. Most remain asleep. Some start crying at some stage or other- for example when the judge is speaking. Miss Elizabeth Page did something new. She needed to be fed at the very second we had to walk to court. She was SCREAMING. Her screams echoed off the office walls, and then in the lift. Her SCREAMS were so bad, and hunger so urgent, that as I tried to compose myself as a lawyer going to court, Roxanne offered to feed her a bottle on the way to court. So there was our little caravan of people: Mitch, Roxanne, Karen, Elizabeth and me, walking to court, while Roxanne carried Elizabeth, who was feeding from a bottle. Elizabeth was too young to have fed a bottle in the stroller as we walked up.

Of course, by the time we got there, she had largely calmed down. Court went well. The judge agreed with my submissions. He said that I was widely regarded as an expert in my field, and that my submissions, as usual, were meticulous. He agreed that Roxanne was the only parent before the making to the parentage order- and made the order. He congratulated us[65].

We had photos in the court room of this amazing event. Roxanne, Mitch and I then went up to Queen Street Mall to have a glass of bubbles. Elizabeth was well behaved.

We suggested to Roxanne to have yum cha. She declined and went shopping instead. Mitch and I then walked with Elizabeth to the car, at which time she had turned into a portable air raid siren. You cannot possibly know how loud a screaming baby is in the confines of a car until you have experienced it yourself. It takes my ears days to recover.

As we drove to our favourite yum cha restaurant in Fortitude Valley, the screaming got WORSE and WORSE. Mitch and I shouted at each other that we would get there and feed or change her straightaway.

Then we saw the most ominous sign: "For lease." The restaurant had closed. Driving on, we pulled into an underground car park, to check on our wailing banshee.

Mitch then said he had to go to the toilet. Off he went. In the hot, semi-darkness, I took off my coat, grabbed a bottle and fed Elizabeth. Then the inevitable happened. And I had to change her too.

Calm fell. After enduring this shock and awe, Mitch and I decided to drive to close to home to our usual café for lunch. All went well. We were sitting in the light, with a beautiful lunch before us. Elizabeth was at peace. I then saw on my white shirt sleeve some of Elizabeth's green poo, deposited there in the darkness of the car park.

I kept eating.

A couple of weeks later, Steve Jackson from *The Australian* phoned me to ask about what was new and interesting in the world of surrogacy. Steve had previously been a producer on 60 Minutes- where I have been interviewed about Australians going overseas for egg donors[66], and about Joe Donor, who I mentioned in **chapter 1**.

I started talking to Steve as to my concerns about Australians undertaking surrogacy in China. I spoke for some minutes. All I could hear was crickets, and then I said:

> *"Look, I should disclose that my husband and I have had a baby through surrogacy in Brisbane. Because of the recent High Court case[67] and the difference in views by judges in Queensland about who is a parent before the making of a parentage order when there is a single surrogate, we had to get a special ruling in our own case."*

He thought that was newsworthy. I said:

> *"I don't think it's particularly newsworthy. It's only our story. I think what's happening in China is much more worrying."*

He said:

> *"Are you kidding? Australia's leading surrogacy lawyer has to have a special ruling in his own case. That's news."*

The story ran with a photograph taken in our house of Mitch, Elizabeth and me.

We were inundated with congratulations. Then I saw from my Facebook timeline there was a photo of me posted. The post was by a prominent anti-surrogacy campaigner who posted:

> *"With one magic wave of a gavel, this child has been forever denied a mother."*

And then the homophobic abuse by those commenting on her post commenced. Jokes were made about our inability to have children. It was also said that evidently we had no knowledge of childcare because of the way we were holding her (the person who posted forgetting or not realising that we were holding her in an unnatural position because we were directed to do so by the photographer). The hatred was horrible and sickening.

A judge told me as to how to respond:

> *"Don't let the haters win."*

A colleague put it more pithily:

> *"Fuck 'em."*

We have put those days behind us. Our daughter has continued to thrive. Every day she has advanced in some amazing way. We are lucky to be parents. Life is grand.

[48] I have not given the name of my ex-wife nor that of my sons for privacy reasons.

[49] https://www.sdfertility.com/

[50] Being a minor surgical procedure, it could go wrong, like any other surgical procedure.

[51] Estimated as at 2016 at $240 million: https://theconversation.com/ideas-for-australia-rethinking-funding-and-priorities-in-ivf-should-the-state-pay-for-people-to-have-babies-57036.

[52] https://www.aph.gov.au/Parliamentary_Business/Committees/House/Social_Policy_and_Legal_Affairs/Inquiry_into_surrogacy/Submissions- submission 39.

[53] https://www.abc.net.au/news/2015-06-26/ivf-rates-expense-fact-check/6573208?nw=0&r=HtmlFragment.

[54] https://www.canstar.com.au/health-insurance/ivf-cost/

[55] Australia and New Zealand Assisted Reproduction Database (UNSW), Assisted reproductive technology in Australia and New Zealand 2019 https://npesu.unsw.edu.au/sites/default/files/npesu/surveillances/Assisted%20Reproductive%20Technology%20in%20Australia%20and%20New%20Zealand%202019.pdf. p.43.

[56] https://www.smh.com.au/politics/federal/car-park-scheme-signed-off-without-any-promise-of-extra-spaces-20210704-p586oa.html.

[57] https://www.theguardian.com/australia-news/2021/nov/07/cost-of-australia-holding-each-refugee-on-nauru-balloons-to-43m-a-year.

[58] https://www.msn.com/en-au/news/australia/average-politician-now-costs-aussies-1million-a-year-after-pay-rises/ar-AATxLs8. https://www.abc.net.au/news/2015-06-26/ivf-rates-expense-fact-check/6573208?nw=0&r=HtmlFragment.

[59] Section 16(2).

[60] There is great information on the Queensland Health website about the benefits of breastfeeding. While not every surrogate can provide breast milk, where it is possible to do so, the benefits are enormous: https://www.health.qld.gov.au/clinical-practice/guidelines-procedures/clinical-staff/maternity/nutrition/breastfeeding/importance.

[61] https://s3-eu-west-2.amazonaws.com/lawcom-prod-storage-11jsxou24uy7q/uploads/2019/06/Surrogacy-consultation-paper.pdf. While Australia's basic framework of surrogacy laws is based on the UK model, there is no movement in Australia at all for pre-birth recognition of the intended parents as the parents. Our policy makers still don't get what surrogacy is about. They assume that the surrogate is the mother- while the UK research tells us what we have seen- that surrogates see the intended parents as the parents, and that surrogates do not see themselves as the mothers. They are merely carrying the child for someone else- even when the surrogacy is traditional.

[62] In 2011 I acted for a husband and wife who had a child born through surrogacy in that hospital. My client's mother was the surrogate. I explained to them that as surrogacy was a new experience for the hospital, that they should discuss it through their specialist with the

hospital first to make sure they were welcomed, had accommodation after the birth, etc. All went smoothly.

[63] https://mobile.abc.net.au/news/2019-07-29/push-to-simplify-international-commercial-surrogacy/11303164?pfmredir=sm&fbclid=IwAR1riH8p5iFlErU4pF0Ey-SuOrwfi48OOiXwG_MJ2FxDL_6Y6JTCpM_EPOg&nw=0&r=HtmlFragment.

[64] Masson v Parsons [2019] HCA 21.

[65] And as to the power of a child. The judge was at a public award I attended. Mitch and Elizabeth were there too. I took the judge over to see Elizabeth, who was by now a toddler. I was called away- and looked back to see the judge on his knees beside Elizabeth- the two of them colouring in.

[66] See: https://www.youtube.com/watch?v=3Z6PKT01pdw.

[67] Masson v Parsons [2019] HCA21.

CHAPTER 3

# WHEN NOT IF

I am thankful to my American colleague Rich Vaughn[68] for two wise pieces of advice about surrogacy:

- The process of surrogacy involves a whole series of boxes being ticked, so that properly done, it can go smoothly. However, if one of those boxes is not ticked, the whole process can go awry.
  - A lawyer advising in surrogacy work has one of three roles:
  - An architect – planning and putting together the whole journey. This is his favourite part of the job.
  - A pilot- for those who know what they want- and to get there yesterday.
  - A cleaner- a role he mentioned he gets too often, cleaning up others' messes.

Similarly, I love being the architect. I dislike being the cleaner. When I am the cleaner, I often think:

> *"Why didn't they get the right advice at the beginning? They could have avoided this mess."*

The cost of cleaning up messes is sometimes much greater than if the surrogacy journey had been properly planned from the beginning. I say it repeatedly elsewhere in this book, but I will say it here- *prevention is better than cure*. Get the right advice at the beginning to save you stress, cost and delay.

Undertaking surrogacy means with certainty that you will become a parent. This can be hard to fathom, particularly for straight couples or single women who have endured round after round, after round, of unsuccessful IVF.

Some years ago, I attended the Fertility Society of Australia conference – as a speaker. When I was filling out the various registration forms, an email came for a free breakfast. I decided to go because it was free and it was breakfast. Silly me. Instead, I spent an hour or so listening to the attributes of a particular medicine which, as a lawyer, had nothing or very little to do with me at all. The standout from this breakfast that caused me almost to choke on breakfast was the doctor selling the attributes of this wonderful medicine – and his patient managed to get pregnant on her $38^{th}$ IVF cycle! I was appalled. The word that came through my mind at that very second was *roadkill*. I thought of the poor couple who had to undergo the rollercoaster of emotion of IVF going up the slope hoping: "*I think I can. I think I can*"; but then on the other side crashing down, and yet having to repeat that process time and time again.

The highest number of times that I've seen a couple undertake IVF was when they came to me after 28 cycles – still unsuccessful. Far too many.

About a decade or so ago I started speaking with American fertility specialists. Some of them were highly critical in private of their Australian colleagues. Cynically, it was suggested by some that the reason that Australian doctors kept promoting endless rounds of IVF was because there was a subsidy from the Australian taxpayer for each round. I don't accept that that's the reason. What I've seen is Australian doctors trying to do the best by their patients – often telling the patients that the chances of success are low, but it might work this time.

The American fertility doctors were saying to me that if a heterosexual couple weren't successful with becoming pregnant after 3-5 rounds of IVF, then they should try surrogacy – it's that simple. They were of course much more familiar with surrogacy, it having started over 30 years ago in the United States. About 10 years ago Australian doctors were not so familiar with surrogacy. In a reaction to the Baby M case in New Jersey (1987) when a surrogacy contract was upheld, Australian lawmakers generally reacted with fear – and in one way or another banned surrogacy in Australia- **see chapter 1**.

Doctors can't be blamed if they haven't had familiarity with surrogacy or for that matter, have ethical concerns about it.

Anyone who doesn't have ethical concerns about surrogacy is a fool or a fraud, or both. Surrogacy is a complex process and it's necessary to ensure that the ethics are right.

Over the last 10 years (with the exception of the 28 cycle couple), I have seen Australian doctors embrace surrogacy more and more.

The reason is simple. Surrogacy is a certainty that you will become a parent. It is when, not if you get there.

There are four exceptions to that, which I have set out in the next chapters, but it is absolutely certain that you will become parents through surrogacy if you don't meet one of those exceptions.

The reason for this is not spin but is borne out by what I have seen in advising in over 1,750 surrogacy journeys[69] since 1988.

At its essence, surrogacy is merely a manifestation of this simple formula:

*egg + sperm + healthy uterus = baby*

There are two differences between surrogacy and standard IVF. For heterosexual couples, standard IVF involves using his sperm and her egg being implanted into her body resulting in a pregnancy. If either of them has infertility or in a combination they have infertility, or even that there is some unexplained infertility, the couple won't get there. They won't have a baby through that process.

Why surrogacy is different from a medical point of view is that if the bits don't work, they can be swapped around. If the intended parents are willing to try, they can have a sperm donor rather than the man's sperm. They can have an egg donor instead of the woman's egg. If the surrogate is unable to get pregnant using the genetic material (and most of the time, according to doctors, this will be the genetic material, not the fault of the surrogate - although she will always blame herself), you get another surrogate.

Each of these steps are tricky – and there are legal issues with them all, but they are doable.

The point is, there is a certain outcome, namely, the birth of a healthy baby.

At this point, I want to have a shout out for fertility doctors, embryologists and those who work in IVF clinics. Self-evidently, I'm not a doctor. I'm a lawyer. I don't know about intricate medical issues. I won't begin to assume that I know how to thaw an egg or how to achieve the intricacies of IVF. Fertility doctors and their associated staff such as embryologists, and nurses, achieve that magic.

However, doctors are not God (just as lawyers are not God). Some clients who have come to me have told me about doctors advising that they have some unexplained fertility and that the doctor *thinks it's* this or *it may be* that. When we are children, going to the local doctor was like visiting God. The doctor would look in each ear and down the throat and up the nose and proclaim, sagely, that we had a cold, or similar. The more and more complex the problem, as infertility is often extremely complex, the more one realises that when doctors do their best, often they are only guessing. Often they don't know. They are using their many years of medical training and years of experience to try and diagnose the problem to then suggest a solution. This is no criticism of doctors, but merely stating the obvious: doing their best, sometimes they simply don't know what the cause of the infertility is.

## THE OTHER DIFFERENCE BETWEEN IVF AND SURROGACY

IVF is only a medical process (albeit a very complex one), while surrogacy is *both* a medical *and* a legal process. Most surrogacy involves IVF, and surrogacy has this legal process to determine that the intended parents are the parents of the child. The intended parents[70] might be recognised as the parents by a transfer of parentage or they might be recognised by operation of law – for example, they might be considered to be the child's natural parents all along, even though someone else, a surrogate, is carrying the child. One of the tricks necessary with surrogacy is to get that legal process right.

The four reasons you won't become parents are, quite simply,

1. You die.
2. You run out of patience.
3. You run out of money.
4. You aren't prepared to use a donor.

I cover these in the next four chapters.

[68] https://www.iflg.net/who-we-are/rich-vaughn-esq/.

[69] (As of late 2021)

[70] It aggravates me that when Australian states decided to talk about those who wanted to be parents they did not all use the obvious, and international term, "*intended parents*", and have used "*substitute parents*" (ACT) (which sounds that they are not the real parents, but fakes), "*arranged parents*" (WA) (which does not give them credit as the driving forces resulting in the birth of their child) and "*commissioning parents*" (which sounds like someone buying a fridge, boat or artwork, and demeaning their role of intending to be the parents.): (Victoria, which confusingly has substitute parentage orders). I hope that "intended parents" is used in future.

CHAPTER 4

# DEATH – THE FIRST REASON YOU WON'T BECOME A PARENT

It sounds pretty macabre that in a book talking about the joy of new life and becoming parents that I'm discussing death. Lawyers of course talk about risk every day of the week. The reason it's important to talk about death is that it could happen. As Benjamin Franklin said over 200 years ago there are two certainties about life – death and taxes. Of course, it's been suggested there is a third, change.

Despite the absolute certainty that all of us are going to die, it has been estimated that about half of all Australians don't have wills[71]. Whether that number's accurate or not, it's essential to have estate planning as part of your surrogacy journey.

All lawyers know that it is essential to have a will. I have lost count of the number of clients who are lawyers, and in one case a judge, who did not have wills. We're all fearful and therefore avoidant of death.

Since 1988 I have advised in over 1,750 surrogacy journeys for clients throughout Australia and many overseas countries. I mention this number a few times in this book. The point is that it's a large number. None of my clients have died during the journey. They could have. In one family where I acted for the surrogate, the reason driving surrogacy was because the intended mother had cancer and therefore a loss of fertility. After the baby was born and parentage of the intended parents established, she died.

In another case, a single dad died about seven years after his child was born.

These deaths could have occurred during the pregnancy or between the pregnancy and when the parents were recognised as the parents.

The last thing you want is to have a child born on the other side of the world or indeed the other side of the country who is left as a penniless orphan – who has no resources available to them and has no legal guardian. In some countries where surrogacy is popular, such as the United States, there will be an estate plan in place. However, this does not cover a will.

Care must be taken also for Australians in executing overseas wills because we don't have estate or death duties, but the overseas place might do, and your family and child may find that a large chunk of your estate is eaten up in taxes that could easily not have had to be paid if proper planning had occurred.

### WHAT IS DEATH DUTY

When a person dies, a percentage of their estate is paid as a tax. Death or estate duty is very efficient, but hated. It remains a common tax in Europe, for example.

In the early 1970s, then Queensland Premier Joh Bjelke-Petersen took the bold step of abolishing death duty in Queensland. The immediate outcome was an enormous number of retirees moving interstate to Queensland, resulting in boom conditions on the Gold Coast. The secondary result? All other states then abolished death duty as well.

### THE THREE KEY STEPS TO PROTECT YOUR CHILD

#### 1. Have a Will.

Your Will should be properly drafted and executed. It should make allowance for your unborn child. Get a lawyer experienced in this area to draft it. Don't leave it to chance. Just because you have a will doesn't mean that your child is necessarily protected. Just because you have a lawyer who has acted for you in other matters, if they are not familiar with the issues in surrogacy, they may fail your child. It is important to get specialist's advice in this area. If a will was executed by you before certain key events- your marriage or your divorce, it may no longer be valid.

Back in 1988 I acted for a wife in a family law property matter. She had separated from her husband. My client started court proceedings. On a Friday afternoon, the husband and wife met with their lawyers in tow, trying to reach agreement. We couldn't reach agreement. It wasn't helped when I asked the husband about the ownership of a 50 foot boat. He denied ownership. He said:

*"It's owned by a man in Sydney."*

I knew I was young and green, but I also knew I was being lied to.

Court was on the Monday morning. My client was seeking 60% of everything that was owned, which was almost all in his name. My client called me and told me that she was not going to court. I demanded she come to court, not listening to her. She then explained that her husband had died on that boat on the weekend, and whilst she was sad that he had died, was happy that he had not changed his will, and that she was to inherit 100% of the property! Understandably she did not want to continue with court.

On another occasion, a family law client of mine called me out of the blue. "How are you?" she asked. I told her I was fine. "What can I do to help?"

"Well," she said, "I've just called for an ambulance and am going to hospital for an urgent operation. My doctor says I will lose a bit of blood- and because I am a Jehovah's Witness and therefore won't have a blood transfusion, I have a 60 % chance of death."

I dropped everything I was doing. My associate and I went to the hospital straight away. We witnessed my client (while she was bleeding profusely) execute her will in the hospital bed.

Thankfully she survived.

If you don't have a will, you will die intestate. The law, not you, specifies who gets what when someone dies intestate. In all likelihood the division of your estate won't be how you would have wanted it.

In your Will specify a guardian or guardians for your child. This is someone who is responsible for making legal decisions for your child once they are born. If you have been killed in a traffic accident, you won't be able to. You don't want your child adopted out or members of your family having to deal with a messy family law dispute on the other side of the world or even interstate. Prevention is better than cure. Your will should *always* specify a guardian.

## 2. Life Insurance

If you are eligible for life insurance (and some people due to medical reasons are not) make sure you have an adequate amount of life insurance and that you have properly specified the beneficiary. Please get advice from a reputable and competent financial planner to make sure that you have the right amount of cover and that there is a proper protection of the beneficiaries.

## 3. Nominate a beneficiary for your superannuation

Most of us these days have superannuation (which for non-Australians is compulsory retirement savings). You can have a binding nomination of a beneficiary or a non-binding nomination of a beneficiary. You should get advice from competent financial planner to ensure that there is a nomination of beneficiary to make sure that your child (born or unborn) is protected. Failure to do so could result in messy litigation afterwards when some other family member or friend (such as a former partner) makes a claim on the superannuation.

---

[21] https://www.news.com.au/finance/money/wealth/new-research-reveals-52-per-cent-of-adult-australians-dont-have-a-will/news-story/a93f8904936956b48f7f840195413f9c 52% of adult Australians don't have wills: Finder research, 2018.

CHAPTER 5

# YOU WON'T GET THERE – GIVING UP

Surrogacy is the most complex way to have a baby. International surrogacy is the most complex form of surrogacy. International surrogacy through the Covid pandemic, as we have discovered, has made things even more difficult – though still doable.

Finding a surrogate, entering into an agreement with her, having her fall pregnant and giving birth to a healthy child, and even finding an egg or sperm donor can all be steps where something goes wrong and intended parents give up.

Some people go through the whole surrogacy process very smoothly. Within a year or so they become parents.

Other people are not so lucky. They have difficulty finding a surrogate – **see Chapter 12** or finding an egg donor or they have complex medical or financial issues, or the surrogate doesn't get pregnant, or the surrogate has miscarried it.

Of the approximately 1,750 journeys I have advised in since 1988[72], about half are straight couples, about half are gay couples and then there's a relatively small number of single men, single women, three lesbian couples and occasionally a transgender person.

The people I see give up most frequently are straight couples. It makes sense when you think about it. For a gay couple, there is no other way of becoming a parent except surrogacy (or adoption – **see Chapter 9**). They don't have the accumulated emotional baggage of trying and trying and trying previously to become parents that some straight couples might have.

Back in 2015 I spoke at the Bar Association of San Francisco about surrogacy. Another panelist was a local lawyer and friend of mine, Deborah Wald[73]. She said that there was a fundamental difference between gay couples undertaking surrogacy and straight couples. For gay couples, surrogacy was option A – that was it. For straight couples, it was often option D:

- Option A: sex
- Option B: IVF
- Option C: Egg donation
- Option D: Surrogacy

Therefore, the mindset between intended parents who are gay or straight was remarkably different – with gay couples seeing it as an optimistic journey whereas some straight couples were worn down by the process already.

I will give three examples of when people give up.

Sometimes clients of mine give up when the surrogate has a miscarriage. Miscarriages are very common with pregnancy and more so with children conceived through IVF. I don't know why. I am after all a lawyer, not a doctor – but it is more common. Having a surrogate have a miscarriage is gut-wrenching. If you are determined to get there, you will. However, I have had clients (all straight couples) give up after a miscarriage. It is your journey, not anyone else's. You have to work out how much you can cope with. For some clients, it is the straw that breaks the camel's back. If you think you are particularly vulnerable, go and speak to a fertility counsellor. We are blessed in Australia with very good fertility counsellors who are members of the Australian and New Zealand Infertility Counsellors Association (ANZICA)[74].

The worst I have seen was a couple who were clients of mine who underwent international surrogacy. Their surrogate gave birth at 23 weeks. Doctors advise that there was a 50% chance of their daughter dying in the first night. Each day for them after that was laced with the uncertainty as to whether or not their daughter would survive.

After three weeks their daughter died. The couple then phoned me:

*"What should we do?"*

I said:

> "You can give up. No right-thinking person could ever criticise you for giving up. After all, you've lost your daughter. The worst pain that any parent could ever suffer is the loss of their child. But what you haven't done is raise a child to adulthood – which was always the aim of the exercise."

They responded:

> "How do we achieve that?"

I knew immediately because we were having the phone call that they hadn't given up but were determined to have a child to raise as their own. I said:

> "Grieve, then breathe, and then when you're ready - get back on the bike".

The surrogacy agency was very supportive of my clients at such a terrible time. A year later, the couple had the joyous news of having a baby.

As I have set out in **Chapter 2**, Mitch's and my surrogacy journey was immensely complex. It took longer than most. We had financial and medical issues, a miscarriage, an ectopic pregnancy and then a successful birth, just after our daughter almost died in childbirth. Nevertheless, we were blessed with the birth of our daughter. If we had given up, we would not have got there. Life is grand.

---

[22] To the end of 2021.

[23] https://www.waldlaw.net/.

[24] https://www.fertilitysociety.com.au/professional-groups-anzica-australia-new-zealand

CHAPTER 6

# THE THIRD REASON YOU WON'T GET THERE – MONEY

Although it is said that love makes the world go round, unfortunately money is required to enable you to undertake surrogacy. I have seen it said that those who are intended parents are rich. What I've seen in Australia is far from that. Yes, there are rich people undertaking surrogacy. There are also those I would describe as classic middle class (teachers, nurses, for example) and those who are the typical Aussie battlers.

The cost of surrogacy varies greatly.

If you are undertaking surrogacy domestically in the ACT, Queensland, New South Wales, South Australia and Tasmania then I would estimate the cost between $40,000 and $80,000 assuming you were doing gestational surrogacy through an IVF clinic. I would budget at $70,000 over the approximately 18 months to two years of the journey[75]. This should cover all of the costs of IVF and your legal and counselling fees. Most of that budget is for anticipated IVF costs, especially if you have to undergo multiple IVF cycles, and do not have access to Medicare for doing so.

If you are doing so in Victoria, I would add another $5,000 or so.

If you are doing surrogacy in Western Australia, I would add another $10,000 or so.

Surrogacy in Western Australia requires approval of the Reproductive Technology Council. I am aware of one clinic in Western Australia that charges $10,000 to put the application together to obtain that approval. I am not critical of that clinic. It just goes to show how exacting the process is. Western Australia, alone in the world, also requires the donor and the donor's partner to sign the surrogacy agreement[76]. They therefore must have independent legal advice and counselling – which you pay for.

The cost is slightly higher in Victoria than the other eastern states because there is a requirement to undertake approval from a regulator, the Patient Review Panel. While I have heard horror stories of people getting stuck there (and therefore having to pay expensive legal bills)[77], any applications by my clients to the Patient Review Panel have always gone smoothly and those extra costs have not had to be incurred.

I've been told, and some authorities who should know better assert, that rich people undertake surrogacy. Well, yes they do- but not only rich people. Anyone who would be seen as middle class in Australia can afford surrogacy. If they don't have the funds immediately, they do the usual steps to get there:

- Save up
- Get a loan from a bank
- Rely on the bank of mum and dad (not common)
- Budget carefully so they can pay for it as they go.

In the past intended parents could dip into their superannuation account. However, a couple of years ago the Australian Tax Office (as the entity given the power whether to release that money) decided that intended parents should not be able to do so. However, the ATO allows people to use their super money for their own IVF journey. Go figure.

The vast majority of intended parents from my experience would be classified as middle class. It is a myth to say that only rich people undertake surrogacy.

A risk when money is a bit tight in undertaking surrogacy is to cut corners, especially to go to locations where it is probably best not to undertake surrogacy, or seek to skimp on the needs of the surrogate. My simple advice is to plan carefully. Remember that this is a profound human experience, not just a transaction, and be focused at all times on cherishing your surrogate. She is the one who is really taking all the risks. If you think by going to a more exotic location you are saving money, often you aren't. Every day you have to look in the mirror. Can you look in the mirror that in your desperation to have a child that you have exploited someone else? **See Chapters 11, 14,15,18 and 19**.

## WHY THE COST VARIES

The biggest variant in cost in domestic surrogacy is the cost of IVF. Back in 2011, Surrogacy Australia carried out research which showed that intended parents (mainly straight couples) had undertaken $45,000 in IVF, followed by another $45,000 in surrogacy.

The cost of IVF varies dramatically, depending on whether you are able to receive a Medicare rebate. The number of cycles also vary. If you are able to obtain a Medicare rebate and only one cycle of IVF, then the journey will be considerably cheaper than someone who has had to do three cycles of IVF with no Medicare rebates.

## GOING OVERSEAS

More Australian children are born via surrogacy overseas than in Australia. In some years, more Australian children have been born in the US via surrogacy that in Australia. **See Chapter 10 – Numbers Don't Lie – Going Overseas or Local**. Three popular destinations that Australians have gone to have been:

- United States of America
- Ukraine
- Canada

## USA

The cost of going to the US varies dramatically. One of the big issues to take in account in undertaking surrogacy in the US is the exchange rate. After Covid hit, our exchange rate dropped down to US$0.57, before bouncing back closer to recent historical figures of around US$0.75.

I've calculated these figures on a return journey leaving from home to home based on that on the exchange rate of US$0.75.

Costs within the US varies dramatically. As a current chair of the ART Committee of the American Bar Association, Dean Hutchison from Circle Surrogacy said to the International Federation of Gynecologists and Obstetricians (FIGO) last year, surrogacy to the US is not to one place, but one of 51 places i.e. 50 States and the District of Columbia.

As the former chair of the ART Committee of the American Bar Association, Rich Vaughn, has said, there are hundreds of surrogacy agencies in the US, with over 90 alone in California.

The point I want to make is that the cost varies dramatically. It varies, primarily, as to the cost of three factors:

- IVF.
- Where your surrogate comes from. If she comes from Santa Monica in Las Angeles, it is more likely that she will be more expensive than if she comes from somewhere like Kansas.
- The fees of the surrogacy agency.

If you have an egg donor, then the costs again can vary dramatically, such as whether you go through an egg donor agency or direct through an IVF clinic to find your egg donor. The former is normally more expensive.

My estimate, based on my experience with my clients[78] at US$0.75 is a total cost of between A$145,000 – A$300,000.

Often the biggest risk in doing surrogacy in the US is to make sure you have health care costs nailed down. This requires extreme care. A colleague in the US says in his retainer letter that if there is not the right insurance and something goes wrong, the cost for the hospital might be US$17,000 *per day*.

One of the ways I work with clients is to work out how they can save money but still undertake a quality journey. One of the considerations of intended parents in going to the US is whether they want a quicker journey or a slower (often cheaper) journey. It's a value judgment for intended parents to make. There are many excellent surrogacy agencies.

However, care has to be taken. I talk about risks with surrogacy agencies in **Chapter 19**.

# CANADA

Going to Canada is also viable. The exchange rate, although not guaranteed, between the Australian dollar and the Canadian dollar is much less volatile than that between the Australian dollar and the US dollar. Our dollar is usually close to parity, typically coming at about C$.95.

A typical cost, based on my clients' experience[79] is between A$120,000 – A$140,000. There are many fewer surrogacy agencies in Canada than the United States. In the past at least, there has been a greater delay in waiting for surrogates in Canada than the United States. I discussed more about surrogacy in Canada in **Chapters 11** and **19**.

Insurance is also need for the newborn in Canada. If something goes wrong and insurance is not there, Australian intended parents have been liable for over $200,000 in hospital costs[80].

## UKRAINE

At the time of writing this, the Russian Federation appears intent on about to invade Ukraine, much as it did back in 2014.

In the past, based on clients' experiences[81] I would put the costs estimate of undertaking surrogacy in the Ukraine at about A$100,000.

## OTHER PLACES

It is easy to spend too much on international surrogacy. Unfortunately, there are sharks in the water seeking to take advantage of people desperate to have babies. From time to time clients have told me that they have spent US$100,000 to undertake surrogacy in Mexico or other locations where the cost is not dissimilar to what it could have been in a much lower risk jurisdiction such as Canada, or even slightly cheaper than a cheap journey in the US with a good agency.

[75] The numbers in these budgets come from continued feedback I seek from clients about how much the journey cost them.

[76] This assumes of course that you can find a known donor. If you can't in WA, you will either give up, or more likely go somewhere else to become parents, typically overseas but sometimes interstate.

[77] See also the interim report of the review into ART and surrogacy (2018) from page 145 of 168, found here: https://www.health.vic.gov.au/patient-care/review-of-assisted-reproductive-treatment .

[78] As of late 2021.

[79] As of late 2021.

[80] https://pageprovan.com.au/health-insurance-for-overseas-surrogacy-jouneys-is-essential/.

[81] As of late 2021.

CHAPTER 7

# THE FOURTH REASON FOR GIVING UP – NOT USING A DONOR

Some of us who want to become parents must inevitably have the help of a donor in order to become parents. In order to become parents, gay couples like my husband and me, or single men, need the help of two women – a surrogate and an egg donor.

Lesbian couples or single women need the help of a sperm donor.

Quite simply, if these intended parents do not have the help of a donor, they won't get there.

It is all too common for a straight couple to need an egg donor. I do not know why (and again I am a lawyer, not a doctor) but it is very common to see a heterosexual couple need an egg donor as well as a surrogate.

Occasionally, I've seen intended parents who you wouldn't expect to need to have another donor require one. For example, a gay couple undertaking surrogacy who need a sperm donor, as well as an egg donor and a surrogate. Or a lesbian couple who need an egg donor as well as a sperm donor and a surrogate. As I discovered (**see Chapter 1**) it is not inevitable that you will become a parent through your own DNA. You may not. The decision you have to make is whether you are prepared to rely on someone else's DNA to get there. For single men, gay couples, single women and lesbian couples, the process is obvious – a donor is required. For heterosexual couples, it can be more of an emotional challenge.

How desperately do you want a child? As former chair of the ART Committee of the American Bar Association, Steve Snyder[82] once told me, the test is really simple:

> *"If a baby is placed in your arms and you are told, 'this is your baby' will you accept the baby as your own?"*

Evidently, if you're comfortable to accept the baby as your own, you are comfortable with the intricacies that are involved with egg or sperm donation.

However, if you are not comfortable with accepting the baby as your own, then you won't proceed.

By the time most people talk to me, they have got their head around the fact that they need a donor. Only occasionally do clients tell me that they won't accept a donor. If they can't use their own DNA, they don't want a child.

It's a value judgment that you might have to consider. I ask clients to consider this even though at the beginning of their journey when they see me, they may not need a donor. It should be discussed so that if there is a need to have the assistance of a donor, whatever decision is made has been made however long before – to either go ahead with the donor or not.

Quite simply, if you aren't prepared to use a donor but you need one, you won't get there. On the other hand, if you do need a donor and you are prepared to use one, you will get there.

---

[82] https://www.iarcsurrogacy.com/about-iarc/.

## CHAPTER 8

# JARGON SCHMARGON

The world of IVF is full of jargon. Trying to get your head around the jargon at times can make your head hurt, but still no closer to what you thought.

I have a pretty good vocabulary. I thought I knew my way around the jargon, until one day I had to speak at an IVF clinic's national conference. A previous speaker was talking in so much scientific jargon that I had no idea what she was saying. I wanted to know what the words were that she was describing. So I quickly entered them into my phone and then I Googled them. I particularly wanted to see if they were in the Scrabble Dictionary. Not that I play Scrabble often. I wanted some broad measure to see if the words she was using were widely recognised- and *if* I happened to put one of these words on the board, amongst all the arguments, I would triumph!

One of the words that the speaker used was *trophectoderm*. When I looked *trophectoderm* up on www.scrabblewordfinder.org, the page said:

*"**Not a valid word**."*

Then when I looked up the meaning of trophectoderm online, I got this definition from Merriam-Webster[83]- which explains why I called this chapter jargon schmargon:

*"**trophectoderm**

noun

troph·ec·to·derm | \ ˌtrōf-ˈek-tə-ˌdərm \

**Medical Definition of trophectoderm**

: trophoblast especially : the outer layer of the mammalian blastocyst after differentiation of the ectoderm, mesoderm, and endoderm when the outer layer is continuous with the ectoderm of the embryo"* .

And then I realised what it was. Derm is of course to do with the skin. *Trophectoderm* is in effect the skin of the embryo. Bingo!

So here are some terms that you may come across, and what they mean. Where there is a word used in italics in translation, it is also a term.

| Term | Translation |
|---|---|
| altruistic surrogacy | Where the surrogate is not out of pocket, but does not profit. However, what is altruistic surrogacy varies state by state according to state laws. Altruistic surrogacy may be gestational surrogacy or traditional surrogacy. What may be altruistic surrogacy in one place may be compensated surrogacy or commercial surrogacy somewhere else. For example, paying for a surrogate's travel would be altruistic surrogacy in Queensland but commercial surrogacy in Western Australia. |
| ANZICA | Australian and New Zealand Infertility Counsellors Association. Most counsellors you see in Australia concerning surrogacy will be ANZICA members. However, they may not be. In Tasmania, for example, counsellors for surrogacy must be accredited, but may not have much or any infertility experience. |
| ART, assisted reproductive treatment, assisted reproductive technology, artificial reproductive technology | Depending on who you listen to depends on which form of these words is used. Sometimes this includes artificial insemination, but confusingly sometimes it does not. It is usually seen as the whole kit and caboodle of how to have a baby other than through sex. For example: Assisted Reproductive Treatment Act 1988 (SA), Assisted Reproductive Technology Act 2007 (NSW). |

| | |
|---|---|
| arranged parents | Intended parents, as defined in Western Australia. |
| artificial conception procedure | This is the definition of how a child has come to be born other than via sexual intercourse- as defined under the Family Law Act 1975 (Cth). |
| birth mother | Surrogate. |
| birth parent | Surrogate, surrogate's partner, and sometimes someone else identified by the law as a parent when the child is born. |
| blastocyst | This is a day 5 or day 6 embryo. Clinicians will usually implant a blastocyst as this is seen as the most advanced (and therefore viable) embryo. |
| commercial substitute parent agreement | The term used in the Parentage Act 2004 (ACT) for commercial surrogacy. |
| commercial surrogacy | Where the amount paid to a surrogate is deemed to be commercial, and therefore illegal. What is commercial surrogacy varies state by state (and internationally), so that what might be an altruistic surrogacy arrangement in one state is a commercial surrogacy arrangement in another state. Compensated surrogacy may or may not be commercial surrogacy. Commercial surrogacy may be gestational surrogacy or traditional surrogacy. |
| commissioning parents | Intended parents- as used in Victorian law and by some IVF clinics. |

| | |
|---|---|
| compensated surrogacy | A surrogacy arrangement where the surrogate is compensated in some way- by a fee or payment of the surrogate's expenses. It may or may not be commercial surrogacy. Compensated surrogacy may be gestational surrogacy or traditional surrogacy. |
| conception | This is when a child is conceived. This is such a controversial term (as to whether conception occurs at the time of cell division or pregnancy) that there is not a world consensus on what it means. In a world first in a Queensland case in which I acted for the surrogate[84], the court determined it meant the act of pregnancy. |
| cryopreservation | Freezing through the use of liquid nitrogen of eggs, sperm and embryos. |
| domicile | A legal test to determine a person's permanent home. Someone domiciled in NSW (even if they do not currently live there) can commit offences against the Surrogacy Act 2010 (NSW). See also ordinarily resident. |
| embryo | An egg fertilised by sperm. |

| | |
|---|---|
| extra-territorial laws | Most law is deemed to apply in the place that made the law. However, sometimes the laws apply to an event occurring outside that place, seen in respect of surrogacy in the ACT, Queensland, NSW and Hong Kong. For example, under section 11 Surrogacy Act 2010 (NSW), anyone who is ordinarily resident in or domiciled in NSW who enters into a commercial surrogacy arrangement (as defined under NSW law) commits an offence, even if they do so overseas, and even if it is lawful overseas for them to do so. Extra-territorial laws are similar to long arm laws. See also ordinarily resident and domicile. |
| ethics committee | Some IVF clinics have a separate ethics committee, which is required to approve a surrogacy arrangement before that clinic will undertake treatment. Some do not. |
| gestational surrogate, gestational surrogacy | Where the surrogate carries or gestates the child for someone else and does not have a genetic relationship with the child, unlike traditional surrogacy. Gestational surrogacy may be altruistic surrogacy, commercial surrogacy or compensated surrogacy. |
| hatching, assisted hatching | Where the IVF clinic assists the embryo's shell to be broken, so that cell division can then commence quickly. |

| | |
|---|---|
| ICSI | Intra cytoplasmic sperm injection. If you google IVF, typically you will see a picture of ICSI. This is where one sperm is chosen (typically in cases of low male fertility or surrogacy) in the lab, the tail is snipped off, the head is placed in a tube, another tube holds the egg- the skin or tropechtoderm of the egg is pierced and the sperm is injected, causing fertilisation. The skin of the egg then reseals once the tube is removed from the egg. |
| infertility | A disease characterised by the failure to establish a clinical pregnancy after 12 months of regular, unprotected sexual intercourse or due to an impairment of a person's capacity to reproduce either as an individual or with his/her partner. Fertility interventions may be initiated in less than 1 year based on medical, sexual and reproductive history, age, physical findings and diagnostic testing. Infertility is a disease, which generates disability as an impairment of function. Therefore a single person or a same sex couple may have infertility within this definition. |
| intended parents | Those seeking to be parents through surrogacy. |
| IP's | Intended parents. |

| | |
|---|---|
| IVF | In vitro fertilisation- where the egg is fertilised in glass (hence "in vitro") by sperm. Traditional IVF involves up to 200,000 sperm being placed into a dish holding one egg (an egg is humanity's largest cell, and a sperm cell is the smallest), in the hope that one of them will pierce the skin of the egg (the tropectoderm) and enable fertilisation. ICSI is a form of IVF. |
| long arm laws | These are laws similar to extra-territorial laws. They extend the jurisdiction of the state interstate or overseas, much like a long arm. For example, the effect of section 12 Criminal Code 1913 (WA) means that if the elements of the offence of entering into a surrogacy arrangement that is for reward under the Surrogacy Act 2008 (WA) are committed in WA, then the offence is committed in WA, even though the surrogacy arrangement is lawful overseas where the surrogate lives. |
| oocyte | Egg. Pronounced "oh- a site". |
| ordinarily resident | The place as a matter of fact where someone usually lives- relevant to whether an offence has been committed under extra-territorial surrogacy laws in the ACT, Queensland and NSW. For example, under section 54 Surrogacy Act 2010 (Qld) an offence can be committed anywhere in the world if the person is ordinarily resident in Queensland. See also, for NSW, domicile. |
| parentage order | An order by a court transferring parentage from the surrogate (and her partner if there is one) to the intended parent or parents. This order is made post-birth. |

| parental order | The UK version of a parentage order, made post-birth. |
|---|---|
| parenting order | Confusing jargon! An order made under the Family Law Act 1975 (Cth) about with whom a child lives, who has parental responsibility and who the child spends time with. The order is typically made by the Federal Circuit and Family Court of Australia or by the Family Court of Western Australia. This order does not, unlike a parentage or adoption order, make someone a parent. It governs aspects of parenting, and expires at the latest by the time the child turns 18. |
| parent | The person recognised by law as the parent of a child. The person may or may not be the genetic parent. |
| PGD, PGS and PGT | These are variants on a theme- pre-genetic diagnosis, pre-genetic screening and pre-genetic treatment. In essence this involves removing a few cells from a blastocyst and checking the genetics. Checking is undertaken either to prevent hereditary disease transmission or to determine gender. The latter is generally banned in Australia. For example, genetic selection is banned in Victoria; section 28 Assisted Reproductive Treatment Act 2008 (Vic). |
| pre-birth order, PBO | An order made in many parts of the United States recognising someone as a parent, often made at about 4 months gestation. |
| PRP | Patient Review Panel of Victoria- the statutory body that approves surrogacy arrangements through IVF clinics |

| | |
|---|---|
| quarantine | To avoid transmission of disease, especially HIV, IVF clinics often provide for the embryo to be frozen, and then blood tests run again after a period, before the embryo can be used. This period is called quarantine. |
| RTC | Reproductive Technology Council of Western Australia- the statutory regulator of surrogacy in WA, and approves imports into and exports out of WA of donated gametes and embryos. |
| second parent adoption order or step parent adoption order | When the first parent is recognised as a parent but the second is not, recognition is obtained by one of these orders. The crossover with adoption is confusing. These are commonly used in parts of the US and can be available in some circumstances in Australia[85]. |
| spermatazoa | Sperm. |
| substitute parents | Intended parents, as used under ACT law. |
| substitute parents agreement | Surrogacy arrangement. |
| substitute parentage order | Term used in Victorian law for parentage order. |
| surrogacy arrangement that is for reward | The term used in the Surrogacy Act 2008 (WA) for commercial surrogacy. |

| | |
|---|---|
| surrogate, surrogacy | A surrogate is a person who gives birth to a baby for someone else, the process being called surrogacy. The forms of surrogacy are: altruistic surrogacy, commercial surrogacy, compensated surrogacy, gestational surrogacy, traditional surrogacy. |
| surrogate mother | Surrogate. |
| thawing | The complicated process of enabling a frozen embryo is brought to room temperature. It is quite unlike putting a frozen chicken on the sink to defrost. |
| traditional surrogate, traditional surrogacy | Where the surrogate is the genetic parent of the child, unlike gestational surrogacy where she has no genetic relationship with the child. Traditional surrogacy is unable to be done in some places, and some clinics may refuse to do it because of perceived higher risk. In Victoria, for example, while traditional surrogacy is able to be done at home, it cannot be done through an IVF clinic: section 40(1)(ab) Assisted Reproductive Treatment Act 2008 (Vic). Traditional surrogacy may also be altruistic surrogacy or commercial surrogacy or compensated surrogacy. |
| VARTA | Victorian Assisted Reproductive Treatment Authority- one of the regulators of the IVF industry in Victoria, and approves imports to and exports from Victoria (including interstate) of donated gametes and embryos. |

| vitrification | Where an egg, sperm or embryo is snap frozen so that it can be stored in liquid nitrogen, typically by placing the egg, sperm or embryo in close contact with super chilled metal. The egg, sperm or embryo then instantly turns into a glass like substance, i.e. it vitrifies. |

---

[83] https://www.merriam-webster.com/medical/trophectoderm.

[84] LWV v LMH [2012] QChC 26- see Chapter 1.

[85] For example in Re Blake [2013] FCWA 1 http://www8.austlii.edu.au/cgi-bin/viewdoc/au/cases/wa/FCWA/2013/1.html, where a gay couple had undertaken surrogacy in India but only one of them had been recognized as a parent. The step-parent adoption order enabled the other parent to also be recognized as a parent.

CHAPTER 9

# WHAT ABOUT ADOPTION?

There are only two ways for someone to become a parent through a court order- adoption or surrogacy. While a parenting order under the *Family Law Act 1975* might give someone parental responsibility, it does not make them a parent.

Adoption is different to surrogacy. Adoption involves the transfer of an existing child from the parent or parents (if there are parents) to the adoptive parents, usually by court order. Surrogacy on the other hand is the conception and birth of a child created due to the actions of the intended parent or parents to reproduce.

Confusingly, in some places the process of adoption can overlap with surrogacy:

- Sometimes, especially in some US states, such as Hawai'i or Minnesota, the process of surrogacy often involves a second parent adoption. Care needs to be taken that there is not a breach of the various laws across Australia for paying for the adoption. These laws, such as section 303 of Queensland's *Adoption Act 2009*, apply in some circumstances to overseas adoptions.
- Sometimes, the parents might come back from overseas where only one is recognised (as the surrogate is recognised there as the mother, such as parts of Mexico, or where only one man in a gay couple is recognised as entering into the surrogacy agreement there, such as used to occur in India), so the parties want to obtain a step-parent adoption here. Great care must be taken before making application to the court, in case a criminal offence was committed here.
- Sometimes, the parties have undertaken a domestic surrogacy arrangement but it is non-compliant. One of the parties is recognised as a parent, but the other is not- in which case they might consider obtaining a step-parent adoption order. The legal costs in doing so

might far exceed those if they had a compliant surrogacy arrangement. A consistent message in this book is: *prevention is better than cure.*
- In some overseas places, for example, Florida, New Zealand, Nigeria and Kenya, the process of surrogacy is sometimes or always regulated by adoption.

However, I want to focus on adoption as an alternative to surrogacy. I have lost count of the number of times hopeful parents to be have told me:

> *"We were thinking about helping an unfortunate child through adoption, rather than doing surrogacy, but when we looked adoption seemed depressing."*

The picture of adoption in Australia is pretty gloomy. The process of adoption is a lot cheaper than that of surrogacy. Most of the costs are met by the State. However, the numbers are depressing. According to the Australian Institute of Health and Welfare[86], there were 264 adoptions finalised in Australia in the year ended 30 June 2021, which it describes as: *"the lowest number on record"*.

The Institute records that in 1997 there were 709 adoptions in Australia, when according to the Australian Bureau of Statistics Australia had a population of 18.52 million. The population in Australia in 2021 was 25.7 million. To convert what this means in reality, in 1997 one in 26,121 people were adopted, whereas in 2021, one in 97,348 were adopted. In other words, for every adoption that occurred in 2021, four occurred per capita in 1997.

The breakdown of the statistics of adoptions is even more depressing.

## AUSTRALIAN ADOPTIONS 2021

| Type | NSW | VIC | QLD | WA | SA | TAS/ACT/NT | AUST. |
|---|---|---|---|---|---|---|---|
| Known | 122 | 1 | 7 | 34 | 12 | 7 | 183 |
| Local | 12 | 14 | 7 | 4 | 2 | - | 39 |

| Intercountry | 12 | 3 | 16 | 6 | 1 | 4 | 42 |
| Total Adoptions | 146 | 18 | 30 | 44 | 15 | 11 | 264 |

That 264 is a stark contrast to when the shameful processes of adoption occurred in the early 70's. The number of adoptions peaked in 1971-1972 at 9,798[87], (admittedly before the rise of IVF) and has been in decline ever since.

Of those 264 adoptions, 183 or 69% were known child adoptions:

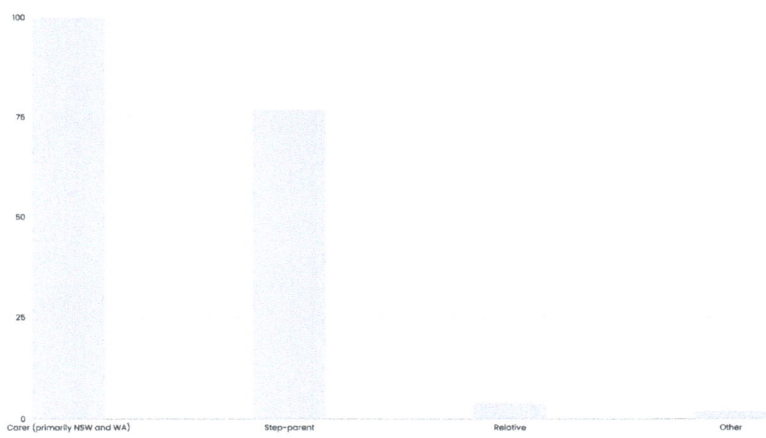

In other words, the number of children who were adopted by people not known to them was 31% or 81 children.

Of the 42 children adopted by intercountry adoption, 38 were from Asia (South Korea 12 and Thailand 16, primarily) and 4 from Central and South America.

None of those countries in which overseas adoption occurred are LGBTIQ+ friendly. No adoptions occurred from Europe, North America or Africa.

What is clear is that if it weren't for carer adoptions (primarily NSW and WA), the numbers would be even more depressing. A rough comparison is that compared to those 81 children who were adopted, approximately 284 children were born via surrogacy, either in Australia or overseas.

Adoption is not quick. According to the Australian Institute of Health and Welfare, in 2020-21, the median length of time from when an adoptive parent became an official client of an Australian State or Territory department, responsible for intercountry adoption to when a child was placed for adoption was three years and four months. The median length of time varied across country. Placements from South Korea had a median time of 24 months, while the median time for the Philippines was over five years.

---

[86] https://www.aihw.gov.au/reports/australias-welfare/adoptions.

[87] Australian Bureau of Statistics, Australian Social Trends 1998, p.33 https://www.ausstats.abs.gov.au/ausstats/subscriber.nsf/0/CA25687100069892CA256889001FBB89/$File/41020_1998.pdf.

CHAPTER 10

# HOW NUMBERS DON'T LIE – OVERSEAS OR DOMESTIC?

Australians go all over the world for surrogacy. This reflects that we are a nation of migrants. The Australian Bureau of Statistics estimates that about half of us are either migrants (from almost every country on earth) or the children of migrants[88]. This rate of migrants is apparently the highest in the Western world[89].

Hence, there are many places across the globe where intended parents have gone to for surrogacy. Some of the countries that my clients have contemplated surrogacy have been places where they have come from, including Bangladesh, Brazil, China, Columbia, Ghana, India, Iran, Kenya, Malaysia, Nigeria, Russia, South Africa, Ukraine and United States. For most of these places, there are small numbers of Australians who go there. Australians who have gone to those places feel comfortable with the systems in those countries. They are wise getting legal advice in Australia before they do so. They may unintentionally commit a criminal offence here. Their journey may be more complex, slower and more costly than they expected.

> **GETTING STUCK – CHINESE STYLE**
>
> Husband and wife had migrated to Australia from China. China does not allow dual citizenship. They had therefore given up their Chinese citizenship when they had become Australian citizens. Feeling comfortable about doing surrogacy in China, they returned back to China to undertake surrogacy. Twins were born. Surrogacy is not illegal in China for intended parents, but it is for the doctors. It is therefore conducted in a grey zone. The parents never got to know the surrogate. After the children were born, they found that the Australian Government refused to grant the children citizenship, because the children's identity was

> not able to be confirmed. *Five years* after the children were born, the children remained in China and the parents in Australia. The children weren't even together. One child was cared for by a grandmother in one part of China and the other child cared for by the other grandmother in another part of China.
>
> If the intended parents had got advice at the beginning, they could have avoided this mess.

As can be seen, international surrogacy births have for a decade always exceeded domestic surrogacy births:

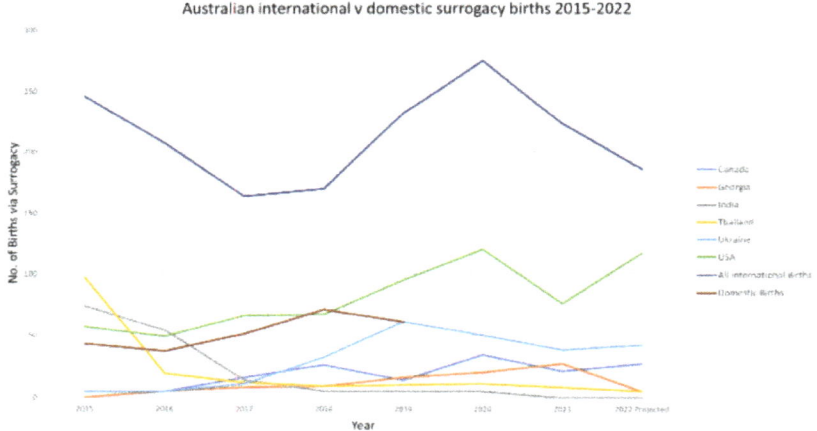

In the 2021 year, the top places that Australians go to for surrogacy have been these:

In 2019, the most recent year for domestic figures, the comparison of international and domestic surrogacy is as follows:

### INTERNATIONAL V DOMESTIC SURROGACY BIRTHS, 2019

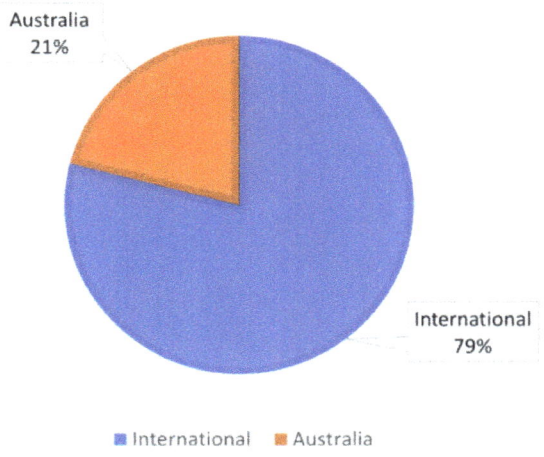

It now appears that more Australian children are born in the United States via surrogacy each year than are born in Australia:

|  | 2018 | 2019 | 2020 | 2021 |
|---|---|---|---|---|
| Australia | 71 | 61[90] |  |  |
| USA | 67 | 95 | 120 | 76 |

The top 5 overseas countries in 2021 were:

| Ranking | Country | No of Australian children born via surrogacy |
|---|---|---|
| 1. | USA | 76 |
| 2. | Ukraine | 38 |
| 3. | Canada | 28 |
| 4. | Georgia | 27 |
| 5. | Mexico | 9 |

**My projections for overseas surrogacy births in the year ended 30 June 2022[91]:**

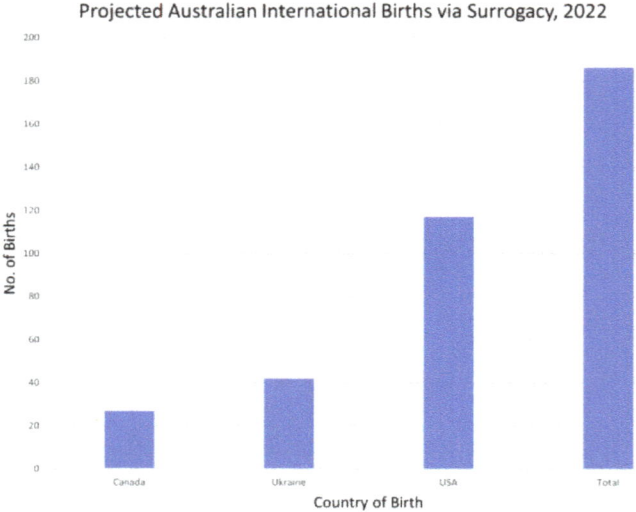

Other than the US or Canada, I do not recommend any of these countries as a general rule. **See chapters 14, 18 and 19**. Great care must be taken wherever intended parents go not to commit offences in Australia as to egg donation or surrogacy – **see chapter 20 for the ACT, chapter 22 for NSW, chapter 23 for Queensland, chapter 24 for SA and chapter 27 for WA**.

There are two sources for this data. When Australian intended parents seek to apply for citizenship for their child, they must apply to the Department of Home Affairs. The Department says that there were 223 applications in the year ended 30 June 2021. This is roughly consistent with previous years, for example, 232 births in 2019 financial year and 275 births in the 2020 financial year.

Domestic births are a bit harder to work out. A unit of the University of New South Wales, the Australian New Zealand Assisted Reproductive Database[92], keeps data on births through Australia and New Zealand IVF clinics. This includes the number of births through gestational surrogacy. There are four issues with the figures from ANZARD in that:

- They don't capture births from traditional surrogacy (where the surrogate is the genetic mother) and therefore capture only the births through clinics.
- They are two years behind, the most recent year being the calendar year ending 31 December 2019.
- They don't give a breakdown between Australia and New Zealand.
- The Department's figures are for the year ending 30 June, whereas ANZARD is for a calendar year. They are always 6 months out from each other.

In the 2019 year there were 73 births through gestational surrogacy in Australia and New Zealand IVF clinics. If Australians and New Zealanders undertake surrogacy at the same rate domestically, then based on population, the proportion of those that are Australian domestic births are 61. The total international births in the year ended 30 June 2019 was 232. The most recent comparison is therefore – 79% of children born through surrogacy are born overseas and 21% born in Australia. Or to put it another way, for every child born in Australia via surrogacy, almost 4 children are born overseas via surrogacy.

Australian intended parents vote with their feet. They recognise the reality that unless you have a surrogate who is a friend or relative, it can be very hard to find a local surrogate. Provided that they pay the right amount of money they can undertake surrogacy overseas.

A reminder of what Sir David Attenborough said:

*"So animals and ourselves, to continue the line, will endure all kinds of hardship, overcome all kinds of difficulties, and eventually the next generation appears."*

Our laws make it an offence for a surrogate to be paid a fee for surrogacy (at the time of writing, excluding the Northern Territory) and this is unlikely to change any time soon. Who would want to risk death or injury for a stranger if you aren't being compensated?

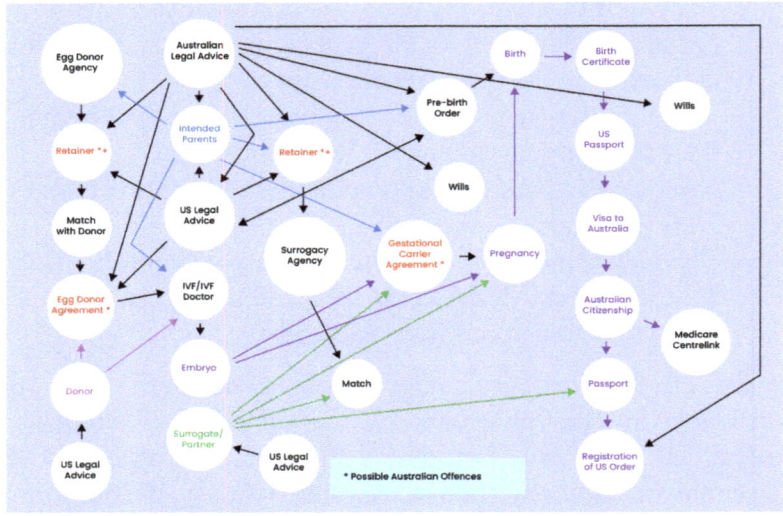

COST A$145,000 –A$300,000 at $A1 = US$0.75
A$167,000-A$346,000 at $A1 = US$0.65

TIMEFRAME: 18-24 months or at worst up to 4 years

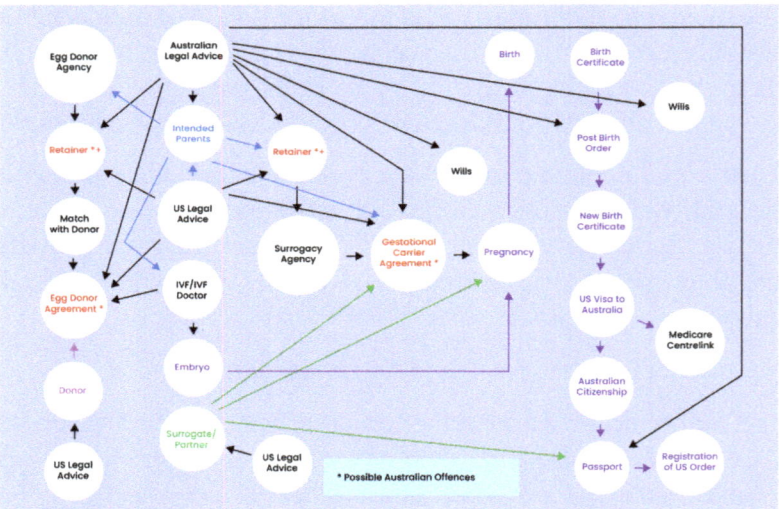

COST A$140,000 –A$300,000 A$1 = US$0.75
A$167,000 –A$346,000 A$1 = US$0.65

TIMEFRAME: 18-24 months or at worst up to 4 years

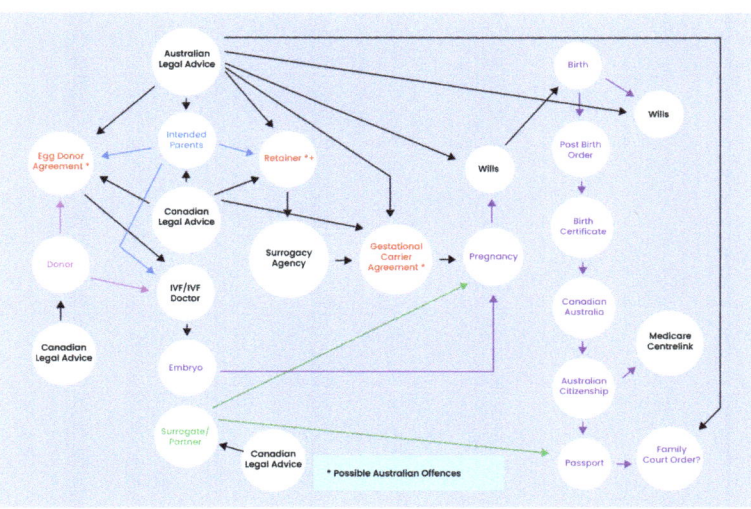

COST A$120,000-A$140,000(Approx)     TIMEFRAME: 18-24 months or at worst up to 4 years

---

[88] In 2020, 7.6 million of us, or 29.8% are migrants form almost every country on earth: Australian Bureau of Statistics, Migration, Australia: https://www.abs.gov.au/statistics/people/population/migration-australia/latest-release . In 2016, according to the Census, a further 20.9% of us had one or both of our parents born overseas.

[89] https://en.wikipedia.org/wiki/Foreign-born_population_of_Australia#cite_note-auto1-3.\

[90] Most recent

[91] Based on the latest figures I have obtained from the Department of Home Affairs, for the period 1 July 2021 to 31 October 2021.

[92] Disclosure: although I am a lecturer at the University of New South Wales, I have no connection with ANZARD.

CHAPTER 11

# LEGAL ISSUES ABOUT GOING OVERSEAS

Once the decision has been made to undertake surrogacy overseas, there are evident serious legal issues. They fall into several categories:
- Criminality.
- Citizenship and passports.

I've also covered criminality separately under surrogacy for each Australian state and territory. Have a look at:
- **Chapter 20 ACT**
- **Chapter 22 NSW**
- **Chapter 22 Northern Territory**
- **Chapter 23 Queensland**
- **Chapter 24 SA**
- **Chapter 25 Tasmania**
- **Chapter 26 Victoria**
- **Chapter 27 Western Australia**

In broad terms, it can be a criminal offence punishable by up to 15 years imprisonment to pay an egg donor other than her reasonable expenses. There are three sets of laws that Australians must navigate for any overseas egg or sperm donation:
- *Prohibition of Human Cloning by Reproduction Act 2002* (Cth).
- The equivalent legislation in every State and the ACT (the NT does not have a human cloning law), for example, Queensland's *Research Involving Human Embryos and Prohibition of Human Cloning for Reproduction Act 2003* (Qld).
- Human tissue laws, for example, *Human Tissue Act 1983 (NSW) and the Transplantation and Anatomy Act 1979* (Qld).

These laws can apply overseas (for example, the Commonwealth law applies to international trade and commerce) or by what is known as a longarm law under State law which applies the States' offences overseas in some circumstances (for example, section 10C Crimes Act 1900 (NSW)) (see what a long arm law is in **chapter 8 Jargon Schmargon**).

Long arm laws apply to either human cloning or human tissue laws or both for residents of:

- ACT
- NT
- NSW
- Queensland
- SA
- WA

Only people living in Victoria or Tasmania do not have to navigate their State's human cloning or human tissue laws because those States do not have a longarm law. Nevertheless, the *Prohibition of Human Cloning for Reproduction Act 2002* (Cth), which carries a 15 year jail term, still needs to be considered for Victorian and Tasmanian residents.

Some of my clients have first sought advice about surrogacy overseas *after* they created embryos there- and were then shocked to learn that they had committed offences with a maximum term of imprisonment of 15 years.

As I say elsewhere in this book, prevention is better than cure. It is better to get legal advice at the beginning of the journey, rather than just later on.

## SURROGACY LAWS OVERSEAS

If that weren't complex enough, five out of Australia's eight jurisdictions make it illegal to go overseas for commercial surrogacy in some circumstances:

- **ACT- for more detail, chapter 20**
- **NSW - for more detail, chapter 22**
- **Queensland - for more detail, chapter 23**

- **SA - for more detail, chapter 24**
- **WA - for more detail, chapter 27**

There is some chatter that it's only illegal if you are from the ACT, Queensland and New South Wales. That's not true. Queensland, the ACT and New South Wales are, with Hong Kong, the only places *in the world* that make it illegal to go overseas for commercial surrogacy.

South Australia and Western Australia also carry risk. This is because they have longarm laws (section 5G *Criminal Law Consolidation* Act 1935 (SA) and section 12 *Criminal Code 1913* (WA)) that extend South Australian and Western Australian jurisdiction in some circumstances. It can be an offence in each place to engage in commercial surrogacy overseas.

At the time of writing (early 2022) not one person has ever been prosecuted for these offences. Nevertheless, the offences remain. They are likely valid law. The offences carry real bite (for example, in New South Wales the offence for entering into or offering to enter into a commercial surrogacy arrangement is a fine of $110,000 or two years imprisonment or both) and could, if there are prosecutions, aside from a fine or jail, result in the loss of that person's livelihood or their profession. As a lawyer I must tell my clients to obey the law.

In some circumstances it is legal if you live in Queensland or, New South Wales in particular, to engage in surrogacy in the United States. This was made plain in a Family Court case in 2016 where the judge held that the US surrogacy arrangement was not commercial but altruistic under both NSW and Queensland's *Surrogacy Acts*[93].

Surrogacy in Canada is altruistic, but it can be considered to be commercial in some circumstances under laws in most Australian states.

It is critical that you get expert legal advice right at the beginning if you're contemplating undertaking surrogacy overseas. Going overseas for surrogacy is like tip toeing through a minefield. Getting expert legal advice at the beginning is a case of prevention is better than cure.

## BUT THAT'S NOT ALL

If you are ordinarily resident (**see chapter 8 Jargon Schmargon**) in the ACT, New South Wales or Queensland but live somewhere else at the moment, you can still commit the offence under ACT, New South Wales or Queensland law.

If you are domiciled in New South Wales (**see chapter 8 Jargon Schmargon**) but live somewhere else, you can still commit the offence in New South Wales. In my view, this is an extraordinary overreach by the New South Wales Parliament, but nevertheless the law remains.

---

### EXAMPLE OF DOMICILE

Bill and Ben had lived in New York for 5 years. Bill got a job there on a work permit, which is a temporary visa. Bill was born in Sydney. Until he moved to New York, Bill had lived his entire life in Sydney. Ben was also born and raised and lived all his life in Sydney, but relying on Bill's temporary visa in the US, applied for and obtained a Green Card in the US. Ben was therefore entitled to live in the US permanently.

Bill and Ben wanted to undertake surrogacy. Bill's domicile, namely his legal home i.e. where he lived permanently, was New South Wales. Ben's legal home i.e. where he lived permanently, was New York.

Because Bill remained domiciled in New South Wales (although temporary resident in New York) the surrogacy agreement had to comply with New South Wales law or on the face of it Bill would be committing an offence in New South Wales.

Because Ben was not ordinarily resident or domiciled in New South Wales, he did not have a direct issue about making the agreement New South Wales compliant.

---

## Coming home

The process of coming home has varied. At the time of writing (February 2022), the process is to obtain Australian citizenship for your child overseas, then an Australian passport, then fly home.

The application for citizenship is made to the Department of Home Affairs. It can be made through a migration agent. Some clients want to do so themselves. The essence of the application is to show that on the date of the child's birth the child had an Australian citizen parent. Who is a parent is not limited to genetics. It is someone seen in the wider view of Australian society to be a parent. However, if there is not a genetic link the Department can view the application with the "utmost scrutiny", to use its words, to avoid child trafficking.

If you are doing surrogacy overseas and know there is not going to be a genetic link, it is wise to plan it carefully from the beginning to have clear evidence once the child is born that you are a parent. I can't emphasise enough that if you happen to be a parent who has lodged an application for citizenship when there is no genetic link, you should be planning from the beginning to have evidence of parentage at the end. Get advice right at the beginning! As I have kept repeating in this book: prevention is better than cure.

Typically, if you go to a developing country or post-Soviet country, expect to prove the genetic link, to a DNA lab approved by the Australian government, such as Identilab[94]. Life then becomes very interesting for you if you then discover (despite what the overseas IVF clinic has told you) that there is no genetic link (as has happened to clients of mine who, against my advice, underwent surrogacy in a developing country).

If you go to the US or Canada, typically you will rely on a court order made there to establish parentage. While in Illinois, Ontario and British Columbia an order is not required (because as a matter of law you are recognised as a parent), from an Australian point of view it is much wiser, in my view, to obtain an order. Part of the reason is to do with passports.

While citizenship is handled by the Department of Home Affairs under the *Australian Citizenship Act 2007* (Cth) passports are handled by the Department of Foreign Affairs and Trade, under the *Australian Passports Act 2005* (Cth). Everyone who is required to consent to the issue of a passport for a child is everyone who has parental responsibility. DFAT takes the view that the surrogate being the birth mother (but oddly, not her partner as a birth parent), is such a person. Therefore, ordinarily she has to fill out a DFAT Form B5 to consent to the issue of a passport. DFAT don't take the same view when a parentage order is made in Australia. In the view of DFAT, the only parents are the parents under the Australian parentage order- not the surrogate.

I always suggest that the surrogate fills out the form B5 after the child is born, even if only as a back up plan.

It doesn't matter if the law overseas is quite clear that the surrogate is not a parent after the court order was made, and indeed in some places was never a parent. DFAT is firm in its position.

> Kyle and Kent Stewart[95] were an Australian couple who lived in Vancouver. Under British Columbia law, they were the parents, without the need to obtain a court order. As they discovered, DFAT would not grant a passport without the surrogate's consent, as it viewed her as the natural mother, despite the law of BC making plain that she was not a parent.

DFAT used to issue passports to children born overseas via surrogacy when the intended parents were named as the parents, and the surrogate was not. Then about 5 or so years ago, they changed – and insisted that surrogates consent to the issue of a passport, and if the surrogate didn't, DFAT wouldn't issue a passport.

So it's not enough to get a court order in the US or Canada. It's necessary to have the order also explicitly enable the parents to take the child overseas or have a passport issued. The reason is an obscure piece of regulation that allows a passport to issue in those circumstances, even if the person with parental responsibility has not consented. I always insist, if I get a copy of the draft order before it is made, to have that clause or clauses inserted.

Why? Because apart from when a passport is lost and has to be replaced, or when a child changes their name, a child's passport only lasts 5 years. It therefore has to be issued- at birth and ages 5, 10 and 15, if the parents want the child to still have the ability to travel overseas. You don't want to have to ask the surrogate to fill out the form B5 each time the passport has to issue if you have a difficult officer from DFAT. Again, prevention is better than cure.

You can always fix this issue with an order under the *Family Law Act*. Ordinarily now there is no need to go to the Federal Circuit and Family Court of Australia or the Family Court of Western Australia as in most cases you will be the parents under Australian law. Get advice from a lawyer here before you start. You want to know as to whether you will be recognised as parents when you come back. The birth certificate is not proof of parentage under Australian law, merely evidence. A lawyer who is experienced in advising about parentage presumptions with surrogacy, like me, can tell you.

Prevention is better than cure.

However, if you have to seek a passport to issue following a court order here, not only will you have to comply with the Court's passport requirements, but also its surrogacy requirements. This involves obtaining an affidavit from the surrogate and from an overseas lawyer, among others. Expect to pay about $25,000 or more to do so.

It is better to save your pennies and plan accordingly.

### The myth of the man with the walrus moustache

When Australians go overseas, especially from the ACT, Queensland and NSW, they fear that on return they will get the tap on the shoulder from an official, and arrested by state police.

Yes, Border Force officials can notify state officials if they suspect that offences have been committed. I am only aware of two cases where Commonwealth officials have notified State officials of possible offences- but ultimately there were no prosecutions.

Our view of how the border works has been framed by films like Titanic- the passengers get off steerage from the ship, land on Ellis Island, where a big fat man in a blue uniform and a walrus moustache determines whether or not they can enter the country. If they fail, they are sent back on the next boat to Europe.

International air travel does not work like that. Before you and your baby get on the plane overseas, you must be cleared by both the overseas government and the Australian government. If there is an issue with your child coming to Australia, it will happen there, for example in Vancouver or LAX, not on arrival in Australia.

I have never seen such a refusal of entry occur overseas or in Australia.

The myth of the man with the walrus moustache is just that-a myth.

---

[23] Re Halvard [2018] FamCA 1051 www.austlii.edu.au/cgi-bin/viewdoc/au/cases/cth/FamCA/2016/1051.html.

[24] https://www.identilab.com.au/

[25] https://www.brisbanetimes.com.au/national/queensland/queensland-family-left-in-limbo-over-passport-debacle-20160715-gq6u4e.html

## CHAPTER 12

# FINDING A SURROGATE

When looking at the numbers and realising that for every child born in Australia, about four are born overseas through surrogacy (see **chapter 10**), it is daunting to consider finding a local surrogate if you don't know anyone. The doyenne of surrogacy counsellors in Australia is Miranda Montrone, in Sydney. She noted that of a sample of 160 surrogacy arrangements over 15 years to 2018, only 5% of the surrogates had been found through online surrogacy forums, most surrogates being primarily close family (sisters or sisters-in-law or mothers) (48.6%) or other extended family or friends (46.3%).

She gives advice on how to find a local surrogate[96].

Ms Montrone says:

> *"There are however consumer non-profit organisations such as Rainbow Families and Gay Dads Australia which are helpful for people wanting to find out about surrogacy. And another, Surrogacy Australia also actively facilitate so many and potential surrogates with intended parents. Note however, that there is a reportedly significantly lower number of potential surrogates that intended parents who are looking for surrogates, so is best not to rely on this method.*
> 
> *Hence, intended parents need to think about finding their surrogate through their own family and friendship networks. This fortunately is not as difficult as often thought, though it may appear to be daunting at the beginning of the surrogacy journey. Experience shows that finding an altruistic surrogacy through networks requires intended parents to calmly, quietly, without emotion or a sense of desperate need, tell everyone that they know that surrogacy is the only way that they can have a baby. As one intended father said 'it is not like you are asking someone for a cup of coffee' and it definitely is not."*

Ms Montrone sets out an example of how intended parents and surrogates find each other:

> *"A woman and her family were on holiday visiting another city in Australia and went to a barbecue organised by friends. There, during conversation, there was discussion of a young extended family member who had a cervical cancer diagnosis just as she had just been planning to start a family. Her world had changed and she and her partner would need a surrogate to have a baby. The visiting woman thought to herself and then said to the family member, 'I have always wanted to be a surrogate'. And from this casual meeting a relationship developed that resulted in a child being born through surrogacy, which connected two families who had previously not been directly connected."*

The Victorian Assisted Reproductive Treatment Authority (VARTA) says this[97] about finding a surrogate:

> *"Finding a surrogate within Australia can seem impossible. It can be difficult to know where to start or who to ask for help. This information can help get you started. You can also contact a counsellor or fertility clinic for advice and support.*
>
> *You should also consider:*
>
> - *Letting family/friends know that surrogacy is your only option.*
> - *Asking a family member or friend for help.*
> - *Seeking a surrogate online through surrogacy support groups or online forums.*
> - *It is illegal to publish an advertisement or notice, or attempt to publicly seek a surrogate. Fertility clinics cannot advertise on your behalf.*
> - *You are not allowed to pay a surrogate other than prescribed costs.*
> - *It is illegal for a surrogate to publicly indicate willingness to act as a surrogate.*

## Things to consider

> *Surrogacy arrangements have many financial, medical, practical and emotional implications for you, your family,*

*and the child born from the arrangement. The laws affecting surrogacy vary across states and territories. You should always seek advice locally to take your individual circumstances into account.*

*It is normal to experience apprehension about needing help, as well as doubts and fear that the surrogate will want to keep the baby or will want to intrude or interfere with your family. In reality, few surrogates do not relinquish the child, with more cases of the intended parent(s) not wanting to take responsibility. In Victoria, the counselling sessions (joint and individual) aim to work through any concerns and potential issues, and ensure everyone is emotionally prepared.*

*Some of the things you should consider include:*

- *Giving yourself time and space to reconcile the grief and loss if you are not going to be genetically related to the child, or are not able to be pregnant and give birth.*
- *There are many avenues to become a parent. Is surrogacy the most comfortable option for you given your circumstances?*

*As with any successful relationship, it takes time to foster good communication, respect and trust between you and a surrogate. Given the complexity of surrogacy, ensure you take time to discuss potential issues and whether to proceed. A shared understanding of expectations and communication for the pregnancy, the birth plan, information exchange and any ongoing relationship with you and the child should be discussed. A surrogacy agreement formalises this and helps all parties clarify their wishes, expectations and responsibilities.*

*The following factors can contribute to a positive surrogacy arrangement:*

- *Stable mental and physical health, a positive life situation, and a supportive partner.*
- *Clear and open communication with clear boundaries and realistic expectations. This is particularly important*

*if you have a pre-existing relationship with your surrogate (i.e. family member, friend).*
- *Trust your surrogate to do the right thing by herself, her body and your baby. Be genuine, respectful, open, reliable and have some degree of flexibility to work well together. Be supportive, build trust by keeping promises and show commitment (e.g. offer practical support, attend appointments, show interest in her health and wellbeing, listen).*
- *Understanding the medical process, success rates and timeframes.*
- *Realistic expectations surrounding emotional changes and reactions that may occur during the process. It is normal to feel anxiety, grief, guilt and disappointment. Be considerate of the potential strain a surrogate is putting on her personal relationships including her family by carrying your child.*
- *Agreeing on reasonable costs which will be reimbursed to the surrogate.*
- *Agreeing on a pregnancy and birth plan that all parties are comfortable with. Keep in mind that the birth mother has the right to manage her own pregnancy regardless of the agreement.*
- *Have common long-term goals about the rights and interests of the child and agreed openness about their conception and genetics.*
- *Be open to ongoing contact and communication in regards to the child. Children often need and like to know their origins."*

I would allow about two years to find a surrogate in these circumstances. This time has to be added to the timeframe for completion of the journey. It is doable, as clients of mine attest, but as Miranda Montrone says, to ask must be done *"calmly, quietly, without emotion or a sense of desperate need"* to everyone they know.

I would describe it as dropping a pebble in a pond and seeing the ripples fan out. If you try this method, you will get there. It just takes time.

Finding a surrogate overseas through an agency is typically quicker. However, yet another impact of Covid-19 has been the way that women who might otherwise considered themselves as possible surrogates have not done so- and as a result there has been a shortage of surrogates in the US. Whether the surrogate is right for you, is another matter.

Whether you are lucky to have a local surrogate or have one from overseas, it is best to get to know them first before leaping in. If your gut is telling you not to go with this surrogate- *trust your gut*! It is best not to end up with a mess. Surrogates with reputable agencies in the US and Canada are thoroughly screened, so the chances of having a fallout with your surrogate are much lower.

The rule of thumb in matching with any surrogate is this, after excluding any crazies:

> *"Is this someone I can be friends with for the next 40 years?"*

Do you don't have to be best mates, or even follow the same football team (or even follow any football)- but is this someone you can relate to and feel comfortable with, knowing that she is potentially putting her life at risk for you, and carrying your child for you- the most precious journey of all? It's not just a transaction, but surrogacy at its best is a profound human experience unlike any other. It's good to get this right.

Pre-Covid, I would encourage my clients to go and visit their surrogate- go to their home and hang out with them. It didn't matter that was on the other side of the world. If you are going to be spending this amount of money and engaging so deeply psychologically, and because of the profound impacts on your child and your family, you want to get this right. With Covid, this has meant instead relying on FaceTime or Zoom, and emails.

I do not encourage intended parents to go to a country where you can't get to know the surrogate. How do you know she is not being exploited? Because the agency or clinic told you so? How can you contact her if and when your child has THAT conversation: *"Where did I come from? How do I meet her?"* If you keep the journey as a secret squirrel experience on a need to know basis- and if your child wants to know, and cannot find out, then aside from any direct impact on your child about not knowing, there could be irreparable damage to the relationship with your child. **See chapter 18**.

As I keep saying in this book: prevention is better than cure.

---

[26] http://www.counsellingplace.com.au/finding-an-altruistic-surrogate/.

[27] https://www.varta.org.au/surrogacy/getting-started-for-intended-parents

CHAPTER 13

# SURROGACY FOR RAINBOW INTENDED PARENTS- AND OTHER DISCRIMINATION

*"Everyone has the right to found a family, regardless of sexual orientation or gender identity. Families exist in diverse forms. No family may be subjected to discrimination on the basis of the sexual orientation or gender identity of any of its members."*

*Principle 24, The Right to Found a Family, Yogyakarta Principles*[98]

If, like me, you are a member of the rainbow community (i.e. LGBTIQ+) then you'll want to know how undertaking surrogacy is different.

### Discrimination under Australian laws

Unfortunately, there remain elements of discrimination in Australian law. Each of the States has its own laws about surrogacy, which I discuss in their own chapters, but I wanted to focus here on the effect of discrimination, and choices for LGBTIQ+ intended parents. At the conclusion of the domestic process (excepting WA and the NT) you'll both be recognised on the birth certificate in Australia as the parents.

See:

- **ACT: chapter 20**
- **NT: chapter 21**
- **NSW: chapter 22**
- **Queensland: chapter 23**
- **SA: chapter 24**
- **Tasmania: chapter 25**
- **Victoria: chapter 26**
- **Western Australia: chapter 27**

## Australian Capital Territory

There is no discrimination based on sexuality in the ACT. Instead, the barriers are that the surrogate must be part of a couple, and the intended parents must be a couple[99]. Luckily, the ACT is not a big place, and there are not the same restrictions in NSW. Moving just across the border can work- but of course you actually have to move: **see chapter 1.**

## Northern Territory

The Northern Territory's *Anti-Discrimination Act 1992* (NT) allows for discrimination in the provision of artificial fertilisation procedures[100]. It's not yet clear whether that provision will be repealed when the Northern Territory legislates for surrogacy, and if not, what actions Repromed[101], the only IVF clinic in the Northern Territory, might take. That provision is also in breach of section 22 of the *Sex Discrimination Act 1984* (Cth).

Because surrogacy can't now occur in a clinic in the NT, the sad reality is that Territorians either go interstate or more likely overseas in their bids to become parents. I long for a time that they have the option of undertaking surrogacy at home.

## New South Wales

No discrimination.

## Queensland

Section 45A of the *Anti-discrimination Act 1991* (Qld)[102] says on its face that it allows Queensland or IVF clinics to refuse treatment based on relationship status or sexuality. It is likely that that section is a dead letter because it runs counter to section 22 of the *Sex Discrimination Act 1984* (Cth) that prohibits discrimination. At the time of writing, Queensland's *Anti-discrimination Act 1991* is being reviewed. Whether s.45A will be abolished remains to be seen.

However, I haven't seen discrimination by IVF clinics in surrogacy in Queensland. A feature of the market in recent years has been Rainbow Fertility[103], which operates in Queensland, New South Wales and Victoria. I was fortunate some years ago to speak at the launches of Rainbow Fertility in Brisbane, Sydney, Gold Coast and Lismore. I thought it important that an IVF clinic stood up and said it actively supported LGBTIQ+ people in their attempts to become parents.

Most IVF doctors that my clients have dealt with are rainbow friendly. In my view, there are four likely reasons for this:

- Discrimination is against the law.
- Doctors want to uphold their Hippocratic oath to do no harm, and are committed to help their patients.
- City Fertility launched its clinic, Rainbow Fertility, specifically targeting members of the rainbow community, which I mentioned above. Several years before they did so, I complained to the managing director of City Fertility Adnan Catakovic that I wished that clinics were much more friendly towards members of the rainbow committee or single intended parents because I was sick and tired of having clients complain to me that if they weren't heterosexual couple, they felt excluded by their IVF clinics. The fact that City Fertility launched Rainbow Fertility and has been a leader in that field, has caused the other major clinics to play catch up and be more friendly to members of the rainbow committee. I

can't claim credit- but I am delighted by their actions to help LGBTIQ+ patients.
- The demand by members of the rainbow community for IVF services, particularly by lesbian couples, remains strong. If you aren't going to service this community, then this will badly impact your profits and profile.

At the 2021 Rainbow Families Queensland[104] seminar, Making Rainbow Babies, three Queensland clinics stood up and supported the event: Rainbow Fertility, Queensland Fertility Group[105] and Life Fertility Clinic[106]. The fact that they did so made plain that IVF clinics, in Queensland at least, are LGBTIQ+ friendly.

## South Australia

IVF doctors under the *Assisted Reproductive Treatment Act 1988* (SA) are prohibited from refusing to provide assisted reproductive treatment on the basis of sexual orientation, gender identity, marital status or religious beliefs, unless the person is a registered objector, in which case the doctor is listed on a public register and must refer the patient to someone else who can treat.

The four IVF clinics in South Australia are:
- Repromed[107] (Monash IVF) – which provides surrogacy including to gay couples
- Family Fertility Centre[108] - which provides surrogacy including to gay couples
- Fertility SA. I do not know if Fertility SA undertakes surrogacy, but this page[109] makes clear that they are comfortable in doing so for same sex couples.
- Flinders Fertility[110]: I do not know if Flinders Fertility undertakes surrogacy.

## Tasmania

There is no discrimination based on sexuality- but everyone signing up to the surrogacy arrangement must reside in Tasmania[111]. This is a barrier to intended parents, given the small and aging population[112], and does not allow flexibility when a family member or friend who is a would be surrogate lives interstate.

## Victoria

No discrimination.

## Western Australia

For single men and gay couples the choices are:

Take the WA government to court in a constitutional challenge;

- Go interstate;
- Go overseas.
- From my experience, most go overseas, though some occasionally go interstate.

If you are a single man or gay couple living in Western Australia, you can't do surrogacy there[113]. By contrast, a single woman and a lesbian couple can undertake surrogacy in WA. However, the practical difficulty in doing so is to have a known sperm donor- as he and his partner have to be parties to the surrogacy arrangement.

What is unclear is when transgender or intersex people can access surrogacy- if they are a single male or are in a male/male relationship, they cannot, but if they are a single female, or they are identified as female in a straight or lesbian relationship they can.

Sometimes your domestic journey can occur if you move residence to either Queensland or New South Wales – but it is absolutely essential to get really good legal advice at the beginning of your journey. I've handled these types of matters before.

Otherwise, you are either looking at making a challenge to Western Australian laws, saying that they are in breach of section 22 of the *Sex Discrimination Act 1994* (Cth) by denying you treatment. You may be a gambler and want to spend 10s or 100s of thousands of dollars in such a challenge with the possibility of a costs order being made against you if you lose. More likely you will want to spend that money going overseas to have a baby. In doing so, you must take care to not inadvertently commit offences as to egg donation or enter into a surrogacy arrangement that is for reward under the *Surrogacy Act 2008* (WA).

To make things trickier in WA, if you are contemplating undertaking any surrogacy journey overseas, including to Canada (which describes itself as an altruistic jurisdiction) you *cannot* get advice from a WA professional because they may be committing an offence under section 11 of the Surrogacy Act 2008 (WA). It is a crime, punishable by up to 5 years imprisonment, for someone to provide a service knowing that the service is to facilitate a surrogacy arrangement that is for reward. You need to get advice from a lawyer interstate, even for preparing a new will. While Canada is clear in its law that it is an altruistic surrogacy jurisdiction, two common payments to surrogates make plain that if someone living in Western Australia undertakes surrogacy in Canada they put themselves at risk of committing an offence under the Surrogacy Act 2008 (WA):

- Travel. Canada is a big place. Travel is not a permitted expense in WA.
- Snow shovelling. Every Canadian surrogacy agreement I have seen always has a provision for snow shovelling. This is not a permitted expense in WA.

**Discrimination in practice in local clinics?**

In the past, I would be told by clients from time to time about discrimination in their IVF clinic. It wasn't the norm, and was usually inadvertent- asking awkward and non-welcoming questions, or presuming the gender of partners on forms to be filled out. Intersex and transgender people would be asked all kinds of awdward questions.

The feedback I have from clients is that this level of discrimination is rare- and that clinics are keen to help LGBTIQ+ patients have children- whether through surrogacy, or egg and sperm donation. Even discrimination against transmen through clinics a few years ago seems to have gone. Fingers crossed.

IVF clinics are subject to the National Health and Medical Research Council, *Ethical Guidelines on the use of assisted reproductive technology in clinical practice and research* (2017)[114], which in effect operate as licensing conditions. Among the guiding principles in the practice of ART set out in the *Ethical Guidelines* is this[115]:

> *"Processes and policies for determining an individual's or a couple's eligibility to access ART services must be just, equitable, transparent and respectful of human dignity and the natural human rights of all persons, including the right to not be unlawfully or unreasonably discriminated against."*

There is the ability of a member of staff or a student who expresses a conscientious objection to the treatment of an individual or to an ART procedure is not obliged to be involved in that treatment or procedure, so long as the objection does not contravene relevant anti-discrimination laws and does not compromise the clinical care of the patient (e.g. the patient is referred to someone without a conscientious objection and is willing to accept their care).

While each state and territory has its own anti-discrimination laws, the Commonwealth has two key laws to stop discrimination in the supply of ART- and it is likely that the state or territory laws that say otherwise will be overridden, as happened previously when the *Sex Discrimination Act 1984* (Cth) overrode South Australian and Victorian laws preventing ART being supplied to single women[116]. The two key laws are:

- section 22 of the *Sex Discrimination Act 1984* (Cth)[117]
- section 24 of the *Disability Discrimination Act 1992* (Cth)[118].

Section 22 of the *Sex Discrimination Act 1984* (Cth) is clear:

> *"It is unlawful for a person who, whether for payment or not, provides goods or services, or makes facilities available, to discriminate against another person on the ground of the other person's sex, sexual orientation, gender identity, intersex status, marital or relationship status, pregnancy or potential pregnancy, or breastfeeding:*
> 
> a. by refusing to provide the other person with those goods or services or to make those facilities available to the other person;
> b. in the terms or conditions on which the first-mentioned person provides the other person with those goods or

services or makes those facilities available to the other person; or
c. in the manner in which the first-mentioned person provides the other person with those goods or services or makes those facilities available to the other person."

Section 24 of the Disability Discrimination Act 1992 (Cth) affects primarily women who have a medical need for ART:

*"It is unlawful for a person who, whether for payment or not, provides goods or services, or makes facilities available, to discriminate against another person on the ground of the other person's disability:*

a. *by refusing to provide the other person with those goods or services or to make those facilities available to the other person; or*
b. *in the terms or conditions on which the first-mentioned person provides the other person with those goods or services or makes those facilities available to the other person; or*
c. *in the manner in which the first-mentioned person provides the other person with those goods or services or makes those facilities available to the other person."*

## Overseas surrogacy options for LGBTIQ+ intended parents

Most overseas jurisdictions for surrogacy are not available for singles or same-sex couples. Ukraine, for example, requires that the intended parents be a heterosexual married couple, one of whom at least has a genetic link with the child.

Both Canada and the United States have been gay friendly for a long time with surrogacy. Following the US Supreme Court decision in *Obergefell v Hodges* [2015] some places in the US, like Texas were suddenly friendly for gay married couples. **See Chapters 11, 15, 18, 19**.

If you go to a rainbow friendly overseas jurisdiction, such as Canada or the United States, you will both be recognised on the birth certificate as the parents.

Care must be taken going to more exotic locations where there is minimal regulation. For example, if you go to Cancun in the Mexican state of Quintana Roo, the genetic father will be recognised as a parent, but the mother will forever be the surrogate. You will have a baby, but only one of you will be recognised as a parent. To fix this, you might have a temporary fix such as a parenting plan (which I have done for clients) or ultimately a step-parent adoption (if that is available). The latter is slow (in the case of New South Wales, the child must be five years old) and costly (particularly if you have to serve the surrogate documents in English as well as Spanish if she lives in Cancun, for example).

A more extreme example is that of Northern Cyprus (formally the Turkish Republic of Northern Cyprus). Surrogacy is undertaken there- where there are no laws. North Cyprus was invaded by Turkey in the 1970's. It regards itself as a breakaway republic from Cyprus- but Northern Cyprus (which is separated from the rest of Cyprus by the United Nations Line of Control) is not recognized by any country other than by Turkey. Most other countries regard it as a part of Cyprus occupied by Turkey. Surrogacy is available (including for gay couples, where the legal fiction is that it is a single man undertaking surrogacy)- but why would you go there? Yes, it's cheap- but:

- There are no laws regulating surrogacy (and presumably few regulating IVF). It would appear that there are few, if any, protections for the surrogate, intended parents or child. Why would you want to go anywhere where there are not protections for human rights involved in the surrogacy journey? If there are few laws and systems regulating IVF, what is the quality of the IVF?
- The question of law is itself questionable in a "country" that is not recognised by any other than the country that invaded and occupied it.
- Therefore, to have the child leave there is questionable- if you aren't a country, you can't issue passports or visas. Do you have to smuggle your child out?
- Assuming you can get the child out of Northern Cyprus, only one of the dads will be recognised as a parent- as the other parent will be the surrogate. While for heterosexual couples, an adoption process could be used to remove the surrogate as the mother and have

the intended mother to be recognised as the mother, that process doesn't work for a gay couple.
- To have the non-biological dad recognised as a parent requires a step=parent adoption to occur back home, with all the potential costs, delays and stress involved with that process.

A message I give through this book over and over is that it is better to plan this right at the beginning – prevention is better than cure. If you have a choice of going to a place that is well regulated, like the US and Canada, with good quality IVF and clear protections, and you can afford it, why would you go to a developing country where human rights protections may be poor, the Australian officials' experience of surrogacy unknown (assuming there are Australian officials in that country) and the quality of IVF poor or unknown?

Often the cost of going to the developing country is about the same as that to Canada or some of the cheaper options in the US. On a few occasions over the years, clients have told me of the cost when they have gone to more exotic locations. Often that cost is about the same as undertaking the same journey in Canada or slightly cheaper than undertaking the same journey in the US. Why pile on the risk unnecessarily?

**HIV+**

The most uncomfortable question I always ask every client who is starting out on their surrogacy journey is as to their HIV status. I hate intruding into my clients' privacy- but it is necessary to know. I do not want to put the health of the surrogate at risk. If she is being asked to be pregnant and endure the pain of childbirth (with all the associated risks), the least that can be done for her is to know whether the sperm or eggs that are going to be used are HIV positive. Similarly, the clinic needs to know.

Of the about 3500+ clients I have acted for, with about 1750 of them gay men, no more than six have been HIV positive. All of them have been gay men. Put bluntly, the rate of HIV infection among gay intended fathers who I have acted for is very low.

As I said in **chapter 8**, clinics take measures including quarantine to ensure HIV is not transmitted. One of the ways of reducing risk of transmission is to first ask patients about risk factors. However, this can be problematic. In the words of one IVF director to me:

*"A problem about the questionnaires is that so many people lie. When asking a man about whether he has had sex with a prostitute, invariably he says no- but many men have had sex with prostitutes- which is why we test."*

He had a point. It is estimated that almost 1 in 6 Australian men have paid for sex- and those who did so were more likely than other men to smoke (which incidentally is extremely harmful to quality sperm), to drink more alcohol, to have had an STI or been tested for HIV, to have had more sexual partners, to have first had vaginal intercourse before 16 and to have had heterosexual anal intercourse[119].

It is thought that having HIV is a barrier to becoming parents through surrogacy. It's not. There must be full transparency- so the surrogate can give informed consent. There has *never* been transmission of HIV through IVF in the world[120], though it's possible on the statistics, because the number of IVF cycles for seropositive cases is so low.

Having HIV will likely slow down the process, make it a bit more costly, involve more doctors- but it is still doable. Steps taken include:

- Quarantine
- Sperm washing – so the sperm is separated from the seminal fluid in a centrifuge. HIV is in the seminal fluid, but not the sperm itself.
- Reducing risk to ensure the viral load is zero or close to zero.
- Use of a preventer, such as Prep.

Some clinics may decline to assist HIV positive patients. From my experience this has not been based on any issue of discrimination, but based on the technical ability of the clinic.

**Is there a difference in outcomes for children having gay parents v. straight parents?**

I have been skeptical for a long time about studies that said that children who had gay or lesbian parents turned out better than children who had straight parents. Often there seemed to be a small sample size- and arguably the researcher had an apparent bias- wanting to find yes as the answer. Similarly, researchers who had a religious bias- and came up with the opposite outcome. No surprises so far.

It now appears that children who have LGBTIQ+ parents, including kids born through surrogacy, do just as well as other kids, if not better. For example, there is an extraordinary body of research work undertaken by Professor Susan Golombok[121] and her colleagues at the Centre for Family Research at the University of Cambridge which demonstrates this.

Longitudinal, large scale research in the Netherlands separately indicates that children of same sex parents do better than that of heterosexual parents[122]. Some of this seems to be being better off, but some of it clearly applies to anyone who is an intended parent through surrogacy, because of the *"time consuming and costly procedures for same-sex couple of obtaining children"* related to parental motivation and family planning before having children. Having a child through surrogacy is not easy, unlike the one night stand that turned bad, resulting in both parents ending up in the Family Court, arguing over their child[123].

Another possibility as to why kids do better is that same sex couples have to be honest with their children about where they came from (which is also a good lesson for straight couples) – **see chapter 18** - and are much less likely to fall into gender stereotypes in their relationship. If you are upfront with your child that your child was conceived out of a process of love, chances are your child will have hangups about how they were created.

> **Alice Clarke**
>
> Some years ago I was fortunate to talk to Alice Clarke[124], who was the first child born in Australia via surrogacy through an IVF clinic. She recalled that in the school yard she had been teased by a boy:
>
> > *"There's something wrong with you. You were created in a test tube."*
>
> Her put down in response was devastating:
>
> > *"Well how were you created? By your parents having sex?"*
>
> At which point all the kids around her wanted to retch. No one ever wants to think about their parents having sex.

## Why do surrogates prefer gay couples?

Dr Kim Bergman, a psychologist and a founder of Growing Generations[125], a long established surrogacy agency in Los Angeles, presented research some years ago that US surrogates preferred gay couples over heterosexual couples as intended parents. At first I thought that was an odd outcome. I thought that a woman who would want to help other women who could not have children would be the obvious motivator. And then the penny dropped. As Deborah Wald said, in **chapter 1**, by the time heterosexual couples have come to surrogacy, it is often option D. By the time gay couples have come to surrogacy it is option A.

If a woman offers to a gay couple to give them the gift of life, they worship at her feet. Gay couples tend to look after her and will do all they can to make her life better. After all, without her they can never be parents.

For some intended mums, they have endured the emotional scarring and baggage of not being able to get there. Sex didn't work. Nor did endless rounds of IVF. Nor did egg donation. In the meantime, while she is hating her body, all her friends and family are having kids, and talking about them and showing them off endlessly. The pain is enduring. The risk is that an intended mum who has gone through this level of pain tries to micromanage the surrogate, a definite no no.

If you had a choice between a couple who are going to worship and adore you, and someone who is going to make your life a misery, who are you going to choose?

The obvious answer for anyone who is to be an intended parent is not to micromanage your surrogate. Remembering that surrogacy is a profound human experience, not a mere transaction, surrogacy works, in the words of Kim Bergman by three factors being present-:

- Mutual respect
- Flexibility
- Communication

[98] http://yogyakartaprinciples.org/principle-24/.

[99] Section 25 and 26 Parentage Act 2004 (ACT).

[100] Section 4(8) http://www.austlii.edu.au/cgi-bin/viewdoc/au/legis/nt/consol_act/aa1992204/s4.html.

[101] https://repromed.com.au/.

[102] http://www.austlii.edu.au/cgi-bin/viewdoc/au/legis/qld/consol_act/aa1991204/s45a.html.

[103] https://www.rainbowfertility.com.au/.

[104] https://www.rainbowfertility.com.au/.

[105] https://www.qfg.com.au/

[106] https://www.lifefertility.com.au/.

[107] https://repromed.com.au/.

[108] https://familyfertilitycentre.com.au/.

[109] https://fertilitysa.com.au/2017/11/29/what-are-your-fertility-options-as-a-same-sex-couple/.

[110] https://flindersfertility.com.au/.

[111] Section 16(2)(g) Surrogacy Act 2012 (Tas) http://www.austlii.edu.au/cgi-bin/viewdoc/au/legis/tas/consol_act/sa2012139/s16.html.

[112] https://quickstats.censusdata.abs.gov.au/census_services/getproduct/census/2016/quickstat/6?opendocument.

[113] Section 19 Surrogacy Act 2008 (WA) http://www.austlii.edu.au/cgi-bin/viewdoc/au/legis/wa/consol_act/sa2008139/s19.html

[114] Which can be downloaded from here: https://www.nhmrc.gov.au/art.

[115] Guiding principle 3.7.

[116] Pearce v. South Australian Health Commission [1996] SASC 5801 http://www8.austlii.edu.au/cgi-bin/viewdoc/au/cases/sa/SASC/1996/6233.html; McBain v Victoria [2000] FCA 1009 www.austlii.edu.au/cgi-bin/viewdoc/au/cases/cth/FCA/2000/1009.html.

[117] http://www8.austlii.edu.au/cgi-bin/viewdoc/au/legis/cth/consol_act/sda1984209/s22.html.

[118] http://www.austlii.edu.au/cgi-bin/viewdoc/au/legis/cth/consol_act/dda1992264/s24.html.

[119] Rissel, Chris E.; Richters, Juliet; Grulich, Andrew E.; de Visser, Richard O.; Smith, Anthony M.A. (April 2003). "Sex in Australia: Experiences of commercial sex in a representative sample of adults". Australian and New Zealand Journal of Public Health. 27 (2): 191–197. doi:10.1111/j.1467-842X.2003.tb00807.x. PMID 14696710. S2CID 25225114.

[120] https://www.pennmedicine.org/news/news-blog/2017/june/how-hiv-positive-men-safely-become-fathers.

[121] https://www.cfr.cam.ac.uk/directory/SusanGolombok.

[122] https://journals.sagepub.com/doi/full/10.1177/0003122420957249.

[123] The longest case I had of that kind was in and out of the courts for 11 years

[124] https://www.abc.net.au/radio/melbourne/programs/saturdaymornings/libbi-alice-maggie-linda/11597804.

[125] https://www.growinggenerations.com/

CHAPTER 14

# CHOOSING AN IVF CLINIC

**In Australia**

It's pretty easy finding an IVF clinic in Australia. If you don't have one in mind, you can always go to www.yourivfsuccess.com.au and find one. It can help going to Facebook groups to find out who has a good reputation.

Sometimes Medicare rebate is paid for IVF and sometimes it is not, depending on the doctor's view on fertility. However, under Commonwealth law, the Medicare rebate is not payable for surrogacy. **See chapter 2- the box on why won't the taxpayer pay Medicare rebate for surrogacy?** When you undertake your fertility journey, it is obvious therefore that sometimes you may be lucky to be able to claim a Medicare rebate for undertaking IVF, but you may also be unlucky in that if you are doing it immediately as part of a surrogacy journey, there may be no Medicare available.

It is important to have a conversation with the proposed IVF clinic as to whether they undertake surrogacy. Some don't. Surrogacy is not a mainstream product. There are relatively few babies being born via surrogacy and there are technical legal issues to be addressed. Therefore, a clinic may decide not to handle surrogacy matters or an individual doctor may refuse to handle surrogacy matters by way of a conscientious objection or because they view it not being something within their usual area of expertise. When you are obtaining a referral from your GP or contacting the IVF clinic, it is useful to ask these things.

Above all, you want an IVF clinic that is technically good and a doctor who is not only technically a good doctor, but also friendly – has a good bedside manner. Of course, you will also need a referral for both of you (if there are two of you) from your GP.

Typically, but not always, a bulk bill IVF clinic won't handle surrogacy. Only asking will tell.

I have had clients who have had bulk bill IVF clinics create embryos and then had all kinds of drama in having those embryos available to them when they want to undertake surrogacy – because it is not the practice of that clinic to undertake surrogacy.

www.yourivfsuccess.com.au sets out statistics of success with individual clinics. Of course, care must be taken with those statistics because they reflect the clientele of that clinic and the expertise of that clinic. For example, a clinic may have lower success rates because it has older patients.

Those statistics come about because clinics have to send data to the Australian and New Zealand Assisted Reproductive Database (ANZARD)[126] run by the University of New South Wales.

The usual practice in Australia, to minimise risk to the surrogate and to any child that might be born (bearing in mind one embryo could be implanted and split, resulting in identical twins being born), is to implant only one embryo. It is comparatively rare for doctors to implant two embryos. I do not recall ever hearing of Australian doctors implanting more than two – at least in recent years. The same cannot be said of clinics in some overseas countries.

We are blessed in Australia to have high quality IVF clinics that are well regulated. Every Australian clinic must be accredited by the Fertility Society of Australia and New Zealand[127]. As a result, clinics must comply with Ethical Guidelines published by the National Health and Medical Research Council, a government body. The Ethical Guidelines cover surrogacy and many other aspects of treatment, and are demanding as to their requirements to show that information is given to patients, that patients are able to give informed consent, and prescribe as to PGD, surrogacy, egg and sperm donation, and many other aspects of running an IVF clinic.

In addition the Reproductive Technology Accreditation Committee of the Fertility Society of Australia and New Zealand requires clinics to comply with its Code of Practice, and in turn regularly audits clinics. Australian auditors are well regarded, and are often engaged in auditing clinics overseas, due to their exacting manner.

IVF clinics, wherever they operate in Australia, are the subject of a thicket of regulation. Clinics in NSW, SA, Victoria and WA are also subject to further state regulation. IVF doctors have told me consistently that they operate conservatively to make sure they comply with their regulation- and they also operate from the perspective of not wishing to court controversy. Their fear is to be on the front page of the local paper- for all the bad reasons.

## CHOOSING AN OVERSEAS IVF CLINIC

Do not assume for a second that an overseas clinic has the same level of regulation as Australian clinics. Australian clinics are rigorously regulated and audited. In some countries, IVF clinics have next to no regulation at all and are not subject to any rigorous auditing process – or if they are, they fail it, but continue to operate. **See chapter 13**.

While US clinics, for example, have different regulation, they too have a process of having to disclose their success rates, published by both SART (the Society for Assisted Reproductive Technology)[128] and the Centers for Disease Control[129].

Three features of US IVF clinics are:

1. Their business model is to get you in and get you out as quickly as possible. They are very conscious of adverse reviews on Google or Yelp. Feedback I have heard time and time again from clients who have felt like they were treated as numbers by some Australian clinics is that they were treated as people by the US clinics. As some clients have said to me:

   *"It's like comparing chalk and cheese."*

2. Unlike Australian IVF clinics where you are asked to sign a series of consent forms but are typically not asked to sign a retainer agreement with the clinic, with US IVF clinics you will be asked to sign a retainer agreement, along with various consent forms. The paperwork can be huge.

3. With most clinics you could see their outcomes with SART or the CDC by going to the SART and CDC websites. You

will see that some clinics decline to provide that information. If they are not prepared to be transparent with SART or the CDC about their results, will they be transparent with you?

Some US clinics prefer to work with an egg donor agency and others have egg donors associated with their clinic who are also patients of the clinic.

If you are choosing a clinic in a more exotic location, for example, in a developing country or a country in Eastern Europe, then speak to a fertility doctor here about what they know about the quality of the work there. I cover some of these issues in **Chapter 13** and in **Chapter 15, There are Guarantees and Guarantees**.

Do your due diligence carefully. You have to act on reputation. Lawyers like myself, while not doctors, are often well aware about who is reputable and who is not. I for one always want to hear feedback- good, bad or indifferent so I can help future clients.

---

[126] https://npesu.unsw.edu.au/data-collection/australian-new-zealand-assisted-reproduction-database-anzard.

[127] https://www.fertilitysociety.com.au/.

[128] https://www.sart.org/patients/fyi-videos/understanding-the-sart-clinic-report/.

[129] https://www.cdc.gov/art/index.html.

CHAPTER 15

# THERE ARE GUARANTEES AND GUARANTEES

Sometimes I am told that the overseas clinic has guaranteed that the clients will have a baby through surrogacy. Sometimes, the guarantee by the overseas clinic is to keep trying IVF until a child is conceived and born. Just like with any other guarantee, the devil is in the detail.

## UKRAINE AND OTHER POST-SOVIET STATES

It's common practice in the Ukraine to guarantee a baby through surrogacy. How is this achieved? There are a number of ways, but the most common is to implant multiple embryos. If one of them takes, then a baby is likely to be born. The problem about implanting multiple embryos is the obvious – placing the health of the surrogate at risk and the health of the babies at risk.

If more than one embryo becomes an unborn baby, at what point does selective reduction occur?

> ### SIX EMBRYOS IN, ONE BABY OUT
> My clients were an Indian couple living in Australia who underwent surrogacy in India. Their first surrogacy journey was unsuccessful. The surrogate (whom they had never met) had not become pregnant. So they tried again. At the end of the process, they were delighted when a child was born. They then met the surrogate very briefly, before taking steps to ensure that the child was able to return to Australia.
>
> The doctor had implanted six embryos into the surrogate. He had not told my clients that there was anything out of the norm in doing so. I was shocked to hear this news and so I asked the obvious question:

> *"What discussion was there about selective reduction?"*

Selective reduction is to ensure that there is an abortion of one or more of the too many embryos. It would normally arise when too many embryos have been implanted in the first place. For obvious reasons, it's not a step to be taken lightly, and should require full disclosure to the intended parents and the surrogate.

My client responded:

> *"What's selective reduction?"*

Evidently there had never been a discussion by the doctor with the intended parents about selective reduction or the possible implications of six embryos being implanted.

The obvious inference was that there had never been any discussion by the doctor with the surrogate either. The doctor by implanting up to six embryos had placed the life of each unborn child at risk and that of the surrogate at significantly greater and unnecessary risk. Neither of the parents nor the surrogate could be said to have engaged in informed consent when one of the most significant risks taken by a reckless doctor had not been explained to them.

## US IVF GUARANTEE

There isn't anything in the United States like Medicare. When going to an IVF clinic in the United States, you pay the lot, that's what.

US IVF clinics charge in one of two ways. Some charge a per cycle fee, much as occurs in Australia (excluding of course that there is no Medicare rebate) i.e. a different charge for each item with an estimate of the entire fee for each IVF cycle.

The IVF fees in US dollars are not that different to unsubsidised IVF here in Australian dollars.

Some clinics instead run a guaranteed program. They will guarantee that they will continue undertaking IVF on your behalf until you become pregnant and have a child (or in the case of a surrogate that the surrogate does so).

What the IVF clinic is betting is that it gets your surrogate pregnant on the first cycle. Some of the statistics of pregnancy for surrogates on the first cycle in these clinics are extremely high. What the clinic asks you to pay is approximately two times or more the cost of a cycle. In other words, you pay up front for two cycles with a very low chance that your surrogate won't get pregnant on the first cycle.

If the surrogate gets pregnant on the first cycle, the clinic wins – but you also win by moving fast onto the path of parenthood. You have also paid over the odds for one cycle of IVF.

Some of my clients would rather pay per IVF cycle. Some want the peace of mind from a guaranteed program. It is a value judgment for you to make an informed choice.

CHAPTER 16

# WHO WANTS TO BE PARENTS THROUGH SURROGACY?

In essence, anybody who needs to undertake surrogacy! There are lots of misconceptions, some from supposed authorities, about who wants to do surrogacy. People of all sizes and occupations, gender, sexuality, wealth and relationship status turn to surrogacy because it is the only way that they will become parents- and if it's well done, it works.

I've not yet met any client who wants to do surrogacy who didn't need to do so. As I once explained to a court:

> *"Most people when they want to have children have sex. For some people that doesn't work and they have to engage in the option of last resort, which is that of surrogacy – and run through a battery of doctors, counsellors and lawyers – and then finally receive that the permission or imprimatur of the State"* i.e. a court order.

No one would want to undertake surrogacy unless they absolutely had to. Who wants to open up about their private life, including their inability to have children – to complete strangers, including a lawyer or lawyers? The answer is no one, unless they absolutely have to. Surrogacy is the most complex form of human reproduction. If you can conceive via sex- that's a lot more fun, less stressful and much, much cheaper than surrogacy.

As I said in **Chapter 13** about half my clients over the years have been straight couples, about half have been gay couples and there has been a few single men, single women and some transgender clients, with three lesbian couples.

My clients have come from all parts of Australia and many parts of the world. Their keen desire is to become parents when biology has put barriers in their way. Of the about 900 female clients I have seen about surrogacy, not one of them has said that she desired to do surrogacy to help save her figure. Undertaking surrogacy is a necessity, not a choice.

CHAPTER 17

# WHO WANTS TO BE A SURROGATE?

Surrogacy is not a mere transaction, like buying a burger, but a profound human experience. A woman who is to be a surrogate must contemplate that there is a low risk of death or injury from giving the gift of life to someone else.

The ideal surrogate is:

- **A woman**. Of course, a transman could be a surrogate- but I have never seen it.
- **Who is aged 25 or more**. A surrogate in some parts of Australia can be as young as 18 but in general, 25 is chosen because it is an arbitrary figure where it is seen that the woman has the necessary maturity, including making choices about the size and shape of her family.
- **Who has had all her own children**. In other words, it's known that she is fertile, and doesn't want any more kids (i.e. yours). She knows what's involved with pregnancy and childbirth, although each pregnancy and childbirth is unique. In most parts of Australia she doesn't have to have had children before, but it's wise that she has done so. **See chapters 26 Victoria and 27 Western Australia**. I have had surrogacy arrangements where the surrogacy has not been pregnant before – and approached them very carefully so that the surrogate is not seeking to hang onto my clients' child and she has at least some idea of what she's in for in becoming pregnant and giving birth. I don't want to put a woman at risk unnecessarily where she has a low risk of death for carrying a child for someone else.
- **Who has had uncomplicated pregnancies and childbirth**. I have only seen one case where a woman who had a 24 hour labour subsequently volunteered to be a surrogate. A woman who has had a four hour labour is much more likely to want to be a surrogate. A woman

who has previously needed a C-section will obviously need to get clear medical clearance about whether she is suitable to carry.
- **Who likes being pregnant**. A woman who has violent vomiting every day through her pregnancy is unlikely to volunteer to be a surrogate! I remember my clients who were the surrogate and her husband sitting opposite me in my office. When I discussed this topic, the would-be surrogate said:

    *"Yes, I'm in the pink when I'm pregnant."*

    Her husband said:

    *"Yes, darl. You're sexiest when you're pregnant."*

- **If she has a partner, that her partner is supportive**. There is no point proceeding if the surrogate has an unsupportive partner. If a surrogate is single, then there should be extra measures in place to ensure she is supported on the way through, including counselling if she wants it and bonding with other surrogates, as happens with some surrogacy agencies in the US, like Circle Surrogacy[130], or Canada, like Canadian Fertility Consulting[131] or ANU Fertility[132].
- Above all, she wants to give the gift of life. This is the strong motivating factor- to be able to help other people have children. Surrogates, in the words of psychologist Kim Bergman[133], have a healthy mix of narcissism *("I'm the best person in the world because I can help others have children.")* and altruism *("It is wonderful to give the gift of life to others.")*.

Surrogates are truly amazing women. Like any other woman who is pregnant and gives birth in Australia, they have a one in 20,000 chance of dying from the experience[134]. Our rates of maternal care in Australia are really, really high, but nevertheless the risk of death remains.

There are higher mortality rates overseas. Always ask. Having had to face Roxanne having needed urgent surgery to remove an ectopic pregnancy, - **see chapter 2**- I can say the mind then wonders:

*"What if she dies?"*

And one thing that nearly losing a child through childbirth has taught me, the better the hospital, the likely the better the outcome in case something goes wrong at birth. Both your surrogate and baby should be cherished all through- but especially this moment. Don't take unnecessary risks!

These women volunteer to help someone else achieve parenthood. Even if they are paid for their troubles (as they are commonly in the United States, for example), it's a pretty low amount given the risk to surrogates, as well as all the "*fun*" stuff through surrogacy, including:

- sore backs
- morning sickness, and
- the pain of giving birth.

Surrogates should always be cherished. What they are doing is extraordinary. Everything that can be done to look after them should happen.

Women who are surrogates sometimes feel a loss at the birth of the child. Through the course of the pregnancy, they recognise that the child is not theirs, but that of the intended parents. Psychologically, it's clear to them that they are not mum but physiologically their body says that they are mum. Sometimes they feel the need, as Miranda Montrone has described, of having a hug attack – that they want to see the baby and hug the baby. This doesn't mean that they want to become mum, but just to know that everything is okay.

A surrogate might be a member of family or a friend or a stranger. In my view there is less risk with a stranger than a friend or a distant cousin. The last two have indistinct boundaries about how they fit in. A very close member of family is clear- at all times the starts remain in the firmament. The sister-in-law will always be the sister-in-law and aunt, not mum.

Dealing with a stranger requires an establishment of trust. If you buy a fridge second hand through Facebook Marketplace, aside from checking out the fridge you want to make sure the person you are buying from is trustworthy. Undertaking surrogacy with a stranger where there isnot the medium of a surrogacy agency requires clear boundaries and trust to be established. The risk if something goes wrong is much higher than buying a second hand fridge!

> **The surrogate to avoid**
>
> My clients were very excited. They had found a surrogate through social media. I immediately told them firmly not to proceed with her. They quickly discovered that she was not suitable.
>
> The would be surrogate was on Centrelink benefits. Warning! The prime motivation for surrogacy should not be about money, no matter where she might be in the world.
>
> Then it was discovered she used ice! AVOID! AVOID! AVOID!
>
> Then if that weren't enough, she was insistent that my clients buy her a car for the privilege of being a surrogate. DANGER, WILL ROBINSON! Luckily, they didn't. Aside from the fact that if they bought the car then my clients (and the surrogate) would be committing a serious criminal offence, this alone demonstrated that the surrogate was not interested in helping others, but was primarily motivated by money.
>
> Luckily, my clients pulled out.

[130] https://www.circlesurrogacy.com/.

[131] https://fertilityconsultants.ca/.

[132] https://anufertility.com/.

[133] https://en.wikipedia.org/wiki/Kim_Bergman.

[134] 5 deaths per 100,000 in 2018: Australian Institute of Health and Welfare https://www.aihw.gov.au/reports/mothers-babies/maternal-deaths-in-australia/contents/maternal-deaths-in-australia .

CHAPTER 18

# THE RIGHT TO KNOW

All of us know, or at least believe, how we were conceived. Our conception is unique to each and every one of us. I find it funny when I hear from same-sex couples that fertility counsellors tell them that they have to be open and honest with the child about where the child came from. Self-evidently, if a gay couple or a lesbian couple are the parents, someone else helped create the child. My daughter Elizabeth goes to daycare. She is at a large childcare centre where there are about 100 families. Her family is the only one that I know of which is an out same-sex couple. Hers is the only one where her parents are two dads. She knows it's different. She realised this at **18 months**.

Social scientists have made plain that it's essential to be upfront and honest with your child about where they came from, including the help of any egg, sperm or embryo donor or surrogate. Speak to them at an age-appropriate level. Continue to emphasise to your child that they were conceived through a process of love and as is often said, it takes a village to raise a family. You receive the help of many others to enable your child to be brought into existence.

You and your partner are the only parents. A donor is just that – a donor, and although they contribute the essence of life i.e. vital DNA material, they do not undertake the heavy lifting of parenting.

In Australia, there is a process of deidentification with most donors so that the identity of the donor is not known to the parents – but can be known to the child after the age of 18 years. The child would go to the clinic or in several States to a Government central register to find out the identity of their donor. Then after a process of counselling the child would be able to introduce themselves to the donor. It just wouldn't be a knock on the door out of the blue.

In some countries, such as Ukraine, the donor is anonymous. Neither you nor your child will be told who the donor is. Ever.

In Canada, the donor is able to be identified for the child.

In the US there are three types of donors:

- Anonymous donors – where the child will never be told the identity of the donor. Until about two or three years ago, this was the most popular form of donor.
- Known donors where, typically, a friend or family member is the donor.
- Open identity donors – where the child, after the age of 18, can find out the donor.

Of course, there is no guarantee that the child will want to find out who the donor is, nor any genetic siblings, nor any guarantee that the donor will be around. The donor may be dead, have lost capacity or have disappeared. But all things being equal, the child should be able to find the donor at that time or later.

True anonymity is dead. The rise of databases like [www.ancestry.com](www.ancestry.com) and [www.23andme](www.23andme).com mean that sooner or later the donor will be able to be identified with certainty. Even if the donor can't be identified now, it is only a question of time. Whether it is wise to search for a donor is another question entirely- and may have profound, irreversible effects on you and your child. Speak to a fertility counsellor first before taking this step, so you know the risks.

---

**HOW TO CREATE A MESS OVER GENERATIONS**

Many years ago, I acted in a particularly ugly family law matter where the parents, husband and wife, were arguing about the care arrangements for their children. The matter was one of those that had a life of its own and kept going and going and going. And going.

How it had started was a relatively minor incident between husband and wife, which then quickly spiralled out of control. It was the kind of minor incident that in many marriages parties would just sail on, making adjustments and be together forever. But in this case there was a KABOOM as their marriage blew up.

What was the ultimate cause of all the problems? It had happened years before these parties had ever met.

The night before the woman's 21st birthday, her parents sat her down and said:

> "There's something we need to tell you. You've been adopted."

Until the age of 21, she had always been of the belief that her parents were her parents. They had never told her about the adoption.

This woman felt betrayed by her parents. If she couldn't trust her parents to tell her the truth about who she was and where she had come from, how could she trust anyone else? Hence, the explosive end of her marriage and the incredible damage done as a result to her children and maybe her children's children – all because of the well-meaning efforts by her parents to try and protect her.

They would have been better to tell her much earlier that she had been adopted and how they loved her so much.

## THE WORRIED DOCTOR

About 20 years ago a doctor had been a medical student when his lecturers said to him and his cohort:

> "Righto boys! Contribute your sperm to science."

They were given very strong pressure to be sperm donors.

In those days, sperm donation was anonymous.

Move forward to when he came to see me. This well respected doctor who had a teenage daughter of his own had suddenly out of the blue received a Facebook request message from a lesbian couple with a picture of a teenage boy:

> "This is your son."

There were three possibilities of how they had found him:

- As he suggested, the clinic had leaked. I considered the chances of this happening to be very low. My experience of Australian IVF clinics is that they zealously guard the privacy of their patients – because the risks to the clinic of damage to their reputation and their all too valuable licence would be trashed in a nanosecond. I said that it was most unlikely.
- There had been some chance passing in person or via social media whereby the women had noticed a resemblance between their child and his child. I had seen cases of this occurring in person and via social media. I said this was a real possibility.
- That someone known to him had undertaken a test through www.ancestry.com or www.23andme.com and he had been tracked down that way.

My client rejected that it could have been anything but option 1. He took my advice and went to see a fertility counsellor, who proved very helpful.

Which one was it?

Drumroll. And the answer is – it was option 3. His mother had, unbeknownst to him, put in an Ancestry.com test. The result was that the women were able to track him down definitively as the sperm donor.

Of course, just because you can track someone down as the sperm or egg donor, does not mean that it is wise to do so, particularly before the child wants to find out. It would be wise to discuss the implications with a fertility counsellor first before acting rashly causing results that you will later regret. Once the damage is done, it's done.

## FIONA DARROCH[135]

Fiona was born in 1962 in South Africa. She and her family later migrated to Australia. After her dad died, she discovered to her horror that he was not her biological father. Her parents had lied to her. Fiona then did tests with www.23andme.com and www.ancestry.com. It turns out that the doctor who had provided treatment had provided his sperm. He had obviously seen himself as God. She then found out that she had something like 200 genetic siblings.

To avoid cases like this, Australian clinics have rigorous testing and regulations about the caps on the number of donations.

It shouldn't be assumed that the child will want to know where they came from. Some of her genetic siblings, like Fiona, were extremely keen to know. Others resented any contact from her at all. They didn't want to know. Others were apathetic about the outcome.

---

[135] https://www.theguardian.com/lifeandstyle/2020/sep/22/learning-that-a-fertility-doctor-was-my-biological-father-was-painful-but-on-the-upside-i-have-hundreds-of-new-siblings

## CHAPTER 19

# CHOOSING A SURROGACY AGENCY V. A BOTTLE OF MILK

When we go to the supermarket fridge and buy a bottle of milk, we know that it is safe to drink. There are a raft of regulations to make it so. We take it for granted that the milk will be safe. Buying a bottle of milk is really cheap.

By comparison, hiring a surrogacy agency (which you need when you go outside Australia to places like the US, Canada and Ukraine) is a lot of money. Most have no regulation at all. Some Australian intended parents assume that they are licensed by the government, much like a clinic here.

They're not. While a bottle of milk (which is very cheap) has so much regulation about it, so as to ensure milk is safe to drink, invariably surrogacy agencies are unregulated, even though the amount of money (and emotional commitment) involved is infinitely greater than a bottle of milk. It is easy in moments of desperation to have a child to get baby lust, and be blind to the obvious- when you are desperate to have a child, and seemingly with deep pockets - there can be sharks in the water.

Almost all surrogacy agencies wherever they exist in the world are completely unregulated. It is a case of buyer beware.

Do not assume that because a surrogacy agency has received good reviews on Google that it is in fact good.

One of the biggest surrogacy agencies in the Ukraine, for example, Bio-Tex was investigated in 2018 on allegations that the DNA test it provided to Italian parents was fraudulent. The parents had their child in the Ukraine via surrogacy in 2011. There needed to be a genetic link between one of them and the child to be eligible for surrogacy. They assured Italian media and the Ukraine Government that they had a report from Bio-Tex that there was a genetic link. However, in 2018 they had to undertake another test in Italy. This showed definitively that there was no genetic link.

There have been cases from developing countries where the agency and the IVF clinic are one and the same and despite being told that all is good, there have been cases where there is no genetic link between parent and child (despite being told otherwise).

Most US surrogacy agencies are highly reputable. Nevertheless, care has to be taken there too.

> ### GREED BECOMES HER
>
> Theresa Erickson[136] was a renowned California surrogacy lawyer. She came up with a scheme involving Ukrainian surrogates. In essence, the "surrogates" would be already pregnant. When desperate clients went to Theresa Erickson, she would say something like:
>
> "It's your lucky day. We have a surrogate in the Ukraine where the intended parents have pulled out."
>
> Of course, this wasn't true. She was in fact engaged in baby selling. US surrogates were sent to be impregnated in the Ukraine with embryos from anonymous donors when the women were in their second trimester. Erickson and others offered the babies to prospective parents telling them that the developing foetuses were the result of legal surrogacy arrangements in which the original parents backed out.
>
> Erickson used her fame as a leading reproductive law specialist to win the trust of both the surrogates and intended parents. One surrogate, Kimberly Schooley, told the judge at Erickson's sentencing hearing that she had miscarried and was forced to name and cremate the child by herself. The judge pointed out that under a legal arrangement, the surrogate would have had the support of the intended parents. Theresa Erickson was sentenced to five months imprisonment, nine months of home detention and had to pay a US$70,000 fine.

### RUDY RUPAK

If you meet a surrogacy promotor at a conference in Australia, you might think that they are legitimate. Not necessarily. It is a case of buyer beware. Rudy Rupak is the classic example.

In 2013 I met Rudy Rupak, who was an exhibitor at the Surrogacy Australia conference in Melbourne, promoting surrogacy in Mexico.

I can't say that I am an expert in the area, but he struck me as what might be seen as an archetypal 1970s porn film director. He left me completely cold.

Subsequently, Australia's ABC and the New York Times exposed him for running a fraudulent Ponzi scheme in Mexico whilst trafficking poor Columbian women to Mexico to be surrogates. After he was exposed, he was caught by the FBI and sentenced to 16 months imprisonment for making interstate wire transfers with the intent to facilitate commercial bribery[137].

US Attorney Alana W Robinson said at his sentencing:

> *"The defendant betrayed the trust placed in him by people desperate to have a child. By praying on their vulnerable emotions, he was able to extract more money on the false promise that he was doing everything possible to help them obtain a baby.*
> *To use the dream of parenthood as leverage for obtaining fraudulent proceeds is intolerable and heart breaking."*

### TRUST YOUR GUT

If it sounds too good to be true or you suspect it's dodgy, go with your gut feeling.

Do not engage an overseas surrogacy agency unless you have undertaken due diligence. Do not assume that if you have been referred to an overseas agency that the person referring you is doing it out of the goodness of their heart and in your best interests.

If an Australian lawyer is referring you to an overseas surrogacy agency, they must reveal any payments that have been proposed.

> **UNDER THE COUNTER PAYMENTS**
>
> There are many sales agents with surrogacy agencies. Some of those are easy to spot – when they tell you that they act for a surrogacy agency. You know that they're going to get a fee based on you hiring the agency. This has to be factored into the cost of the agency.
>
> However, there are others who are not so transparent. I've heard consistent reports of some agents charging a fee to referring their clients on to surrogacy agencies – but also receiving an under the counter fee from the agency.
>
> You should always ask someone who is referring you to a surrogacy agency about whether they are getting paid a fee, (separately from you) for that referral.
>
> I have a duty to my client as a lawyer. I do not get paid for referrals. I refer based on acting in the best interests of my clients. I do not pay to get referrals either.

---

[136] https://abcnews.go.com/US/san-diego-women-sentenced-baby-selling-case/story?id=15785854

[137] https://www.laingbuissonnews.com/imtj/news-imtj/rudy-rupak-sentenced-for-fraud/

# CHAPTER 20

# SURROGACY IN THE AUSTRALIAN CAPITAL TERRITORY

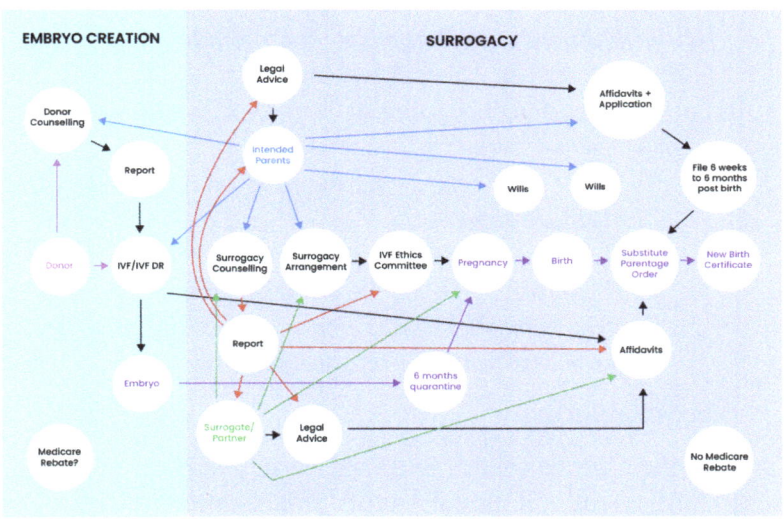

The Australian Capital Territory pioneered surrogacy in Australia, with the passage of the *Parentage Act 2004* (ACT). The Act regulates altruistic surrogacy, but criminalises commercial surrogacy. The Act has also the most restrictive approach to seeking a surrogate, and limits who can seek surrogacy.

**Commercial surrogacy**

Section 41 of the *Parentage Act 2004*[138] (ACT) provides:

*"A person commits an offence if the person intentionally enters into a commercial substitute parent agreement.*

*Maximum penalty: 100 penalty units, imprisonment for 1 year or both."*

It can be an offence, both in the ACT and overseas, punishable by up to 15 years imprisonment to pay an egg, sperm or embryo donor a fee. **See chapter 11.**

## Advertising for a surrogate/ advertising seeking intended parents

Section 43 of the *Parentage Act 2004*[139] (ACT) provides:

1. *"A person commits an offence if the person—*
   a. *publishes an advertisement, notice or anything else with the intention of inducing someone to enter into a substitute parent agreement; or*
   b. *publishes an advertisement, notice or anything else that—*
      i. *is likely to induce someone to enter into a substitute parent agreement; or*
      ii. *seeks or purports to seek someone who is willing to enter into a substitute parent agreement; or*
      iii. *states or implies that someone is willing to enter into a substitute parent agreement.*

   Maximum penalty:

   d. *if the offence relates to a commercial substitute parent agreement—50 penalty units, imprisonment for 6 months or both; or*
   e. *in any other case—50 penalty units.*

2. *In this section:*

   *"publish"—something is **published** if it is—*
   a. *included in a newspaper, periodical publication or other publication; or*
   b. *publicly exhibited in, on, over or under a building, vehicle or place (whether or not a public place and whether on land or water), or in the air in view of people on a street or in a public place; or*
   c. *contained in a document given to someone or left on premises where someone lives or works; or*
   d. *broadcast by radio or television; or*
   e. *electronically disseminated in another way (for example, by inclusion on a web site).*

*Note: An example is part of the Act, is not exhaustive and may extend, but does not limit, the meaning of the provision in which it appears (see Legislation Act)"*

The definition of publish is so wide that placing any notice on any web group (such as a private Facebook group) seeking a surrogate or intended parents is an offence.

## Where are the offences committed?

In the ACT or anywhere else if the person is ordinarily resident in the ACT: s.45 Parentage Act 2004 (ACT)[140].

## What should the budget be for surrogacy in the ACT?

Aim for $70,000. **See chapter 6. See also chapter 2 as to Medicare.**

## How much can a surrogate be paid in the ACT?

She can only be paid her expenses: s.40 *Parentage Act 2004* (ACT)[141] but every case is different.

## Who can access surrogacy in the ACT?

Anyone, provided that they are a couple: sections 24, 25, 26 *Parentage Act 2004* (ACT)[142,143,144]. **See chapter 13**. The surrogate must also be part of a couple: s.24, 26 *Parentage Act 2004* (ACT)[145,146].

## Where can the medical treatment occur?

The child must be conceived as a result of a procedure carried out in the ACT: section 24 *Parentage Act 2004* (ACT). Therefore, it is likely that if the IVF occurs interstate, if the implantation occurs in the ACT, that should be sufficient, but there is no case law on that yet. **See chapter 1 as to the case on conception.**

## Can traditional surrogacy occur?

No: section 24 *Parentage Act 2004* (ACT)[147].

## Does there need to be a genetic link between the parents and child?

Yes- between at least one of the intended parents and the child: section 24 *Parentage Act 2004* (ACT)[148].

### Must the surrogate already have given birth to another child?

No. Even so, IVF clinics may refuse to provide treatment when the surrogate has not.

### How old do the intended parents have to be to enter into the surrogacy arrangement?

18 or older: section 26 *Parentage Act 2004* (ACT)[149].

### How old do the surrogate and her partner have to be to enter into the surrogacy arrangement?

The *Parentage Act 2004* (ACT) is silent on this. While in theory someone under 18 could enter into a surrogacy arrangement, under the *Family Law Act 1975* (Cth) that person's parents absent a court order have parental responsibility, then it is clear that the surrogate and her partner have to be 18 or older.

### Does the surrogacy arrangement need to be written?

No. However, it would be foolish to have an oral agreement. An oral agreement is worth the paper it's written on.

### Does independent legal advice have to be provided before entering into the surrogacy arrangement?

The *Parentage Act 2004* (ACT) is silent on this- but Canberra Fertility Centre[150] has always insisted on this advice being obtained before the clinic gave ethical approval. Genea Canberra[151] and Compass Fertility[152], the two other clinics in the ACT take the same approach.

### Does counselling need to be obtained before the surrogacy arrangement is entered into?

The *Parentage Act 2004* (ACT) requires counselling to have been obtained, but does not say when: section 26[153]. The practice of the clinics is to require the counselling and legal advice to occur before the surrogacy arrangement is entered into- and before pregnancy. The practice of Genea is to require counselling through a clinic counsellor first before attending an independent counsellor.

### Who are the parents when the child is born?

The surrogate and her partner: *Parentage Act 2004* (ACT).

**Who are named on the birth certificate as the parents?**

The surrogate and her partner: *Parentage Act 2004* (ACT).

**Is a post-birth report or counselling required?**

No.

**When can the application be made to the Court for a parentage order?**

Only between when the baby is 6 weeks and 6 months old: section 25 *Parentage Act 2004* (ACT)[154].

**Which court makes the parentage order?**

The Supreme Court of the ACT: section 26 *Parentage Act 2004* (ACT)[155].

**Do we have to physically go to court?**

Yes, subject to Covid.

**Can the baby go to court?**

Check with the court.

**Can photos be taken in the court?**

Check with the court.

**Are the intended parents then the parents for the purposes of Australian law?**

Yes: section 60HB *Family Law Act 1975* (Cth), regulation 12CAA *Family Law Regulations 1984* (Cth)- except if the child is born in Victoria- **see chapter 28 interstate arrangements**.

**Have I acted for clients in the ACT about surrogacy?**

Yes. My first surrogacy clients in the Australian Capital Territory were in about 2008.

[138] http://www5.austlii.edu.au/au/legis/act/consol_act/pa200499/s41.html

[139] http://www5.austlii.edu.au/au/legis/act/consol_act/pa200499/s43.html

[140] http://www5.austlii.edu.au/au/legis/act/consol_act/pa200499/s45.html

[141] http://www5.austlii.edu.au/au/legis/act/consol_act/pa200499/s40.html

[142] http://www.austlii.edu.au/cgi-bin/viewdoc/au/legis/act/consol_act/pa200499/s24.html

[143] http://www.austlii.edu.au/cgi-bin/viewdoc/au/legis/act/consol_act/pa200499/s25.html

[144] http://www.austlii.edu.au/cgi-bin/viewdoc/au/legis/act/consol_act/pa200499/s26.html

[145] http://www.austlii.edu.au/cgi-bin/viewdoc/au/legis/act/consol_act/pa200499/s24.html

[146] http://www.austlii.edu.au/cgi-bin/viewdoc/au/legis/act/consol_act/pa200499/s26.html

[147] http://www.austlii.edu.au/cgi-bin/viewdoc/au/legis/act/consol_act/pa200499/s24.html

[148] http://www.austlii.edu.au/cgi-bin/viewdoc/au/legis/act/consol_act/pa200499/s24.html

[149] http://www.austlii.edu.au/cgi-bin/viewdoc/au/legis/act/consol_act/pa200499/s26.html

[150] https://www.ivf.com.au/clinics/canberra-fertility-clinic

[151] https://www.genea.com.au/clinics/canberra

[152] https://www.compassfertility.com.au/

[153] http://www.austlii.edu.au/cgi-bin/viewdoc/au/legis/act/consol_act/pa200499/s26.html

[154] http://www.austlii.edu.au/cgi-bin/viewdoc/au/legis/act/consol_act/pa200499/s25.html

[155] http://www.austlii.edu.au/cgi-bin/viewdoc/au/legis/act/consol_act/pa200499/s26.html

## CHAPTER 21

# SURROGACY IN THE NORTHERN TERRITORY

There is no surrogacy law in the Northern Territory. In 2021 I was part of the Northern Territory government's surrogacy joint working group. It is likely that there will be a Surrogacy Act in the NT in 2022. I do not know what form the Act will take.

However, as there can be no transfer of parentage, the only IVF clinic in the NT, Repromed, refuses to do any surrogacy work. The clinic is prohibited under the National Health and Medical Research Council Ethical Guidelines from undertaking any commercial surrogacy.

Commercial surrogacy is currently legal in the NT, but must be traditional surrogacy. It is not advised, because of the difficulty in transferring parentage.

Territorians typically go interstate or more commonly overseas to become parents through surrogacy. There are also, therefore, issues about Territory surrogates- who must go interstate well before they are to give birth, so that the intended parents can be recognised as the parents. This either means a flight or a long drive in the Outback.

It can be an offence, both in the NT and overseas, punishable by up to 15 years imprisonment to pay an egg, sperm or embryo donor a fee. **See chapter 11**.

### Advertising for a surrogate/ advertising seeking intended parents

This is currently lawful to do but likely to be outlawed when the news laws take effect.

### Have I acted for clients in the NT about surrogacy?

Yes. My first surrogacy clients in the Northern Territory were in about 2012.

CHAPTER 22

# SURROGACY IN NEW SOUTH WALES

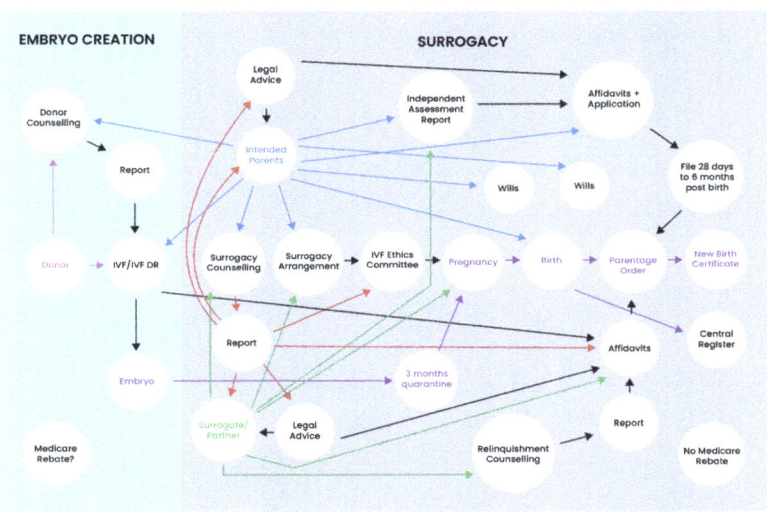

The *Surrogacy Act 2010* (NSW) (and to a lesser extent the *Assisted Reproductive Technology Act 2007* (NSW)) regulates altruistic surrogacy, but criminalises commercial surrogacy.

## Commercial surrogacy

Section 8 of the *Surrogacy Act* (NSW)[156] provides:

> *"A person must not enter into, or offer to enter into, a commercial surrogacy arrangement.*
>
> *Maximum penalty: 2,500 penalty units, in the case of a corporation, or 1,000 penalty units or imprisonment for 2 years (or both), in any other case."*

Money does not need to change hands for it to be commercial surrogacy[157]. It can be an offence, both in NSW and overseas, punishable by up to 15 years imprisonment to pay an egg, sperm or embryo donor a fee. **See chapter 11**.

Advertising for a surrogate/advertising seeking intended parents

Section 10 of the *Surrogacy Act 2010* (NSW)[158] provides:

> *"(1) A person must not publish any advertisement, statement, notice or other material that:*
>
> *(a) states or implies that a person is willing to enter into, or arrange, a surrogacy arrangement, or*
>
> *(b) seeks a person willing to act as a birth mother under a surrogacy arrangement, or*
>
> *(c) states or implies that a person is willing to act as a birth mother under a surrogacy arrangement, or*
>
> *(d) is intended, or is likely, to induce a person to act as a birth mother under a surrogacy arrangement.*
>
> *Maximum penalty:*
>
> *(a) in the case of a commercial surrogacy arrangement--2,500 penalty units in the case of a corporation or 1,000 penalty units or imprisonment for 2 years (or both) in any other case, or*
>
> *(b) in any other case--200 penalty units in the case of a corporation or 100 penalty units in any other case.*
>
> *(2) This section does not apply if:*
>
> *(a) the surrogacy arrangement is not a commercial surrogacy arrangement, and*
>
> *(b) no fee has been paid for the advertisement, statement, notice or other material.*
>
> *(3) In this section,*
>
> *"**publish**" means disseminate or provide access, by any means, to the public or a section of the public.*
>
> **Note** : *See also the Assisted Reproductive Technology Act 2007 which requires providers of assisted reproductive technology treatment to ensure that an assessment report is obtained and considered before a person is provided with treatment in connection with a surrogacy arrangement."*

In other words, if you advertise for an altruistic surrogate, you are not committing an offence- provided either that no money is paid for the ad, or it is in a private group on the web, i.e., it is not to the public or a section of the public.

## Where are the offences committed?

In NSW or anywhere else if the person is ordinarily resident or domiciled in NSW: s.11 Surrogacy Act 2010 (NSW)[159]. **See chapter 11**.

## What should the budget be for surrogacy in NSW?

Aim for $70,000. **See chapter 6. See also chapter 2 as to Medicare.**

## How much can a surrogate be paid in NSW?

She can only be paid her reasonable costs: section 7 *Surrogacy Act 2010* (NSW)[160]. What these are will vary in each case.

## Who can access surrogacy in NSW?

Anyone if they are single or a couple: section 25 *Surrogacy Act 2010* (NSW)[161]. **See chapter 13**.

## Where can the medical treatment occur?

Anywhere. However, there can be practical limitations to this- so it is best to get legal advice on this first. Clients of mine have obtained parentage orders when medical treatment has occurred interstate or overseas.

## Can traditional surrogacy occur?

Yes, however, some clinics, such as IVF Australia, refuse to undertake traditional surrogacy due to perceptions of risk. **See chapter 1**. Clinics such as Monash IVF, City Fertility/Rainbow Fertility deal with traditional surrogacy on a case by case basis.

## Does there need to be a genetic link between the parents and child?

No.

## Must the surrogate already have given birth to another child?

No. Even so, IVF clinics may refuse to provide treatment when the surrogate has not.

## How old do the intended parents have to be to enter into the surrogacy arrangement?

18 or older, but if under 25 their maturity has to be demonstrated: sections 28, 29 *Surrogacy Act 2010* (NSW)[162] [163].

## How old do the surrogate and her partner have to be to enter into the surrogacy arrangement?

Oddly, the surrogate has to be 25: section 27 *Surrogacy Act 2010* (NSW)[164], but there is no age specified for her partner. While in theory someone under 18 could enter into a surrogacy arrangement, under the *Family Law Act 1975* (Cth) that person's parents (absent a court order) have parental responsibility, then it is clear that the partner has to be 18 or older.

## Does the surrogacy arrangement need to be written?

Yes: section 34 Surrogacy Act 2010 (NSW)[165].

## Does independent legal advice have to be provided before entering into the surrogacy arrangement?

Yes: section 36 *Surrogacy Act 2010* (NSW)[166]. There are certain requirements for that legal advice. There are also requirements that some of the clinics, such as IVF Australia, for notification about that legal advice.

## Does counselling need to be obtained before the surrogacy arrangement is entered into?

Yes: section 35 Surrogacy Act 2010 (NSW)[167]. There are also requirements about who can provide that counselling.

The practice of IVF Australia and Genea is to require counselling through a clinic counsellor first before attending an independent counsellor. The practice of other clinics such as Monash IVF and City Fertility/Rainbow Fertility and Fertility First is not.

## Who are the parents when the child is born?

The surrogate and her partner: *Status of Children Act 1996* (NSW).

## Who are named on the birth certificate as the parents?

The surrogate (and if she has one, her partner): *Status of Children Act 1996* (NSW).

## Is a post-birth report or counselling required?

Yes- both an independent assessment and separate relinquishment counselling for the surrogate (and her partner, if she has one): sections 17, 35 Surrogacy Act 2010 (NSW)[168] [169]. There are requirements about who does the assessment and counselling.

## When can the application be made to the Court for a parentage order?

Ordinarily between when the baby is 30 days and 6 months old: section 16 *Surrogacy Act 2010* (NSW)[170].

## Which court makes the parentage order?

The Supreme Court of NSW: section *4 Surrogacy Act 2010* (NSW).

## Do we have to physically go to court?

Ordinarily no, it's done on the papers. However, you can choose to go, subject to Covid.

## Can the baby go to court?

Yes.

## Can photos be taken in the court?

Yes.

## Are the intended parents then the parents for the purposes of Australian law?

Yes: section 60HB *Family Law Act 1975* (Cth), regulation *12CAA Family Law Regulations 1984* (Cth)- except if the child is born in Victoria- **see chapter 28 interstate arrangements.**

## Have I acted for clients in NSW about surrogacy?

Yes. My first clients in New South Wales about surrogacy were in about 2008.

[156] http://www.austlii.edu.au/cgi-bin/viewdoc/au/legis/nsw/consol_act/sa2010139/s8.html

[157] **Application MJC and CSC; re EMC [2012] NSWSC 1626**

[158] http://www.austlii.edu.au/cgi-bin/viewdoc/au/legis/nsw/consol_act/sa2010139/s10.html

[159] http://www.austlii.edu.au/cgi-bin/viewdoc/au/legis/nsw/consol_act/sa2010139/s11.html

[160] http://www.austlii.edu.au/cgi-bin/viewdoc/au/legis/nsw/consol_act/sa2010139/s7.html

[161] http://www.austlii.edu.au/cgi-bin/viewdoc/au/legis/nsw/consol_act/sa2010139/s25.html

[162] http://www.austlii.edu.au/cgi-bin/viewdoc/au/legis/nsw/consol_act/sa2010139/s28.html

[163] http://www.austlii.edu.au/cgi-bin/viewdoc/au/legis/nsw/consol_act/sa2010139/s29.html

[164] http://www.austlii.edu.au/cgi-bin/viewdoc/au/legis/nsw/consol_act/sa2010139/s27.html

[165] http://www.austlii.edu.au/cgi-bin/viewdoc/au/legis/nsw/consol_act/sa2010139/s34.html

[166] http://www.austlii.edu.au/cgi-bin/viewdoc/au/legis/nsw/consol_act/sa2010139/s36.html

[167] http://www.austlii.edu.au/cgi-bin/viewdoc/au/legis/nsw/consol_act/sa2010139/s35.html

[168] http://www.austlii.edu.au/cgi-bin/viewdoc/au/legis/nsw/consol_act/sa2010139/s17.html

[169] http://www.austlii.edu.au/cgi-bin/viewdoc/au/legis/nsw/consol_act/sa2010139/s35.html

[170] http://www.austlii.edu.au/cgi-bin/viewdoc/au/legis/nsw/consol_act/sa2010139/s16.html

CHAPTER 23

# SURROGACY IN QUEENSLAND

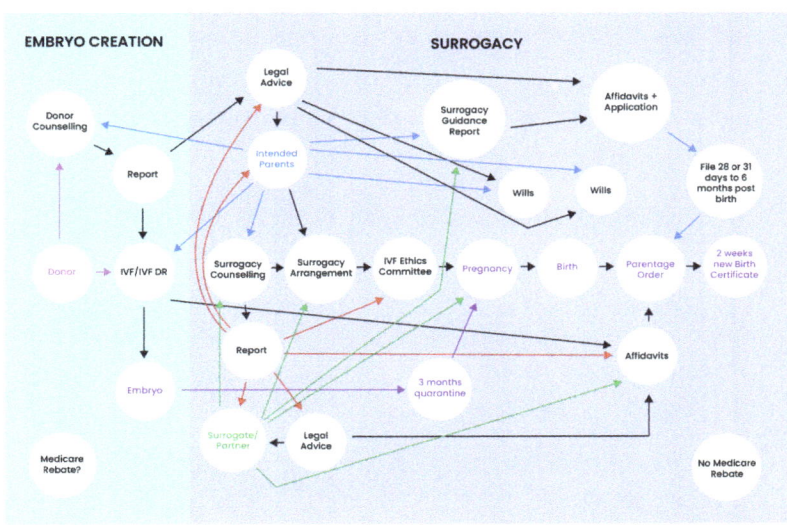

**Commercial surrogacy**

Section 56 of the *Surrogacy Act 2010 (Qld)* provides:

*"A person must not enter into or offer to enter into a commercial surrogacy arrangement.*

*Penalty—*

*Maximum penalty—100 penalty units or 3 years imprisonment."*

While that offence would presumably be committed just once, the next offence can be committed multiple times.

Section 57 of the *Surrogacy Act 2010* (Qld)[171] provides:

*"(1) A person must not give a payment, reward or other material benefit or advantage (other than the reimbursement of the birth mother's surrogacy costs) for another person—*

*(a) agreeing to enter into or entering into a surrogacy arrangement; or*

*(b) giving the intended parent, or intended parents, under a surrogacy arrangement the permanent custody and guardianship of a child born as a result of the surrogacy arrangement; or*

*(c) consenting to the making of a parentage order for a child born as a result of a surrogacy arrangement.*

*Penalty—*

*Maximum penalty—100 penalty units or 3 years imprisonment."*

*(2) A person must not receive a payment, reward or other material benefit or advantage (other than the reimbursement of the birth mother's surrogacy costs) for the person or another person—*

*(a) agreeing to enter into or entering into a surrogacy arrangement; or*

*(b) giving the intended parent, or intended parents, under a surrogacy arrangement the permanent custody and guardianship of a child born as a result of the surrogacy arrangement; or*

*(c) consenting to the making of a parentage order for a child born as a result of a surrogacy arrangement.*

*Penalty—*

*Maximum penalty—100 penalty units or 3 years imprisonment."*

It can be an offence, both in Queensland and overseas, punishable by up to 15 years imprisonment to pay an egg, sperm or embryo donor a fee. See chapter 11.

## Advertising for a surrogate/ advertising seeking intended parents

Section 55 of the *Surrogacy Act 2010* (Qld)[172] provides:

*"(1) A person must not publish an advertisement, statement, notice or other material that—*

*(a) is intended or likely to induce a person to agree to act as a birth mother; or*

*(b) seeks or purports to seek a person willing to act as a birth mother; or*

*(c) states or implies that a person is willing to agree to act as a birth mother; or*

*(d) states or implies that a person is willing to enter into a surrogacy arrangement.*

*Penalty—*

*Maximum penalty—100 penalty units or 3 years imprisonment.*

*(2) In this section—*

*"**publish**" means publish to the public by television, radio, the internet, newspaper, periodical, notice, circular or other form of communication."*

Posting a notice in a private Facebook group, although on the internet is unlikely to be an offence as it is not to the public.

## Where are the offences committed?

In Queensland or anywhere else if the person is ordinarily resident in Queensland: s.54 Surrogacy Act 2010 (Qld)[173].

What should the budget be for surrogacy in Qld?

Aim for $70,000. See chapter 6. See also chapter 2 as to Medicare.

## How much can a surrogate be paid in Queensland?

She can only be paid her reasonable costs: section 11 *Surrogacy Act 2010* (Qld)[174]. What these are will vary in each case.

## Who can access surrogacy in Qld?

Anyone, provided that they are single or a couple: section 21 *Surrogacy Act 2010* (Qld)[175]. **See chapters 1, 13.**

## Where can the medical treatment occur?

Anywhere. However, there can be practical limitations to this-so it is best to get legal advice on this first. Clients of mine have obtained parentage orders when medical treatment has occurred interstate or overseas.

## Can traditional surrogacy occur?
Yes. Clinics such as Queensland Fertility Group, City Fertility/Rainbow Fertility, Monash IVF and Life Fertility deal with traditional surrogacy cases on a case by case basis.

## Does there need to be a genetic link between the parents and child?
No.

## Must the surrogate already have given birth to another child?
No. Even so, IVF clinics may refuse to provide treatment when the surrogate has not.

## How old do the intended parents have to be to enter into the surrogacy arrangement?
25 or older: section 22 *Surrogacy Act 2010* (Qld)[176].

## How old do the surrogate and her partner have to be to enter into the surrogacy arrangement?
25 or older: section 22 *Surrogacy Act 2010* (Qld)[177].

## Does the surrogacy arrangement need to be written?
Yes: section 22 *Surrogacy Act 2010* (Qld)[178].

## Does independent legal advice have to be provided before entering into the surrogacy arrangement?
Yes: section 22 *Surrogacy Act 2010* (Qld)[179].

## Does counselling need to be obtained before the surrogacy arrangement is entered into?
Yes: section 22 *Surrogacy Act 2010* (Qld)[180]. There are requirements as to who is the counsellor to undertake the counselling.

## Who are the parents when the child is born?
The surrogate and her partner: section 17 *Surrogacy Act 2010 (Qld), Status of Children Act 1978* (Qld). **See also Chapter 2**. Following a Family Court case, the Childrens Court ruled in a

case in which I acted for the parents that a single surrogate is the *only* parent before a parentage order is made[181].

## Who are named on the birth certificate as the parents?

The surrogate and her partner: *Status of Children Act 1978* (Qld), with a maximum of two parents: section 10A *Births, Deaths and Marriages Registration Act 2003* (Qld)[182].

## Is a post-birth report or counselling required?

Yes- a surrogacy guidance report as to the best interests of the child: section 32 *Surrogacy Act 2010* (Qld). There are qualifications specified for the report writer.

## When can the application be made to the Court for a parentage order?

Ordinarily between about 30 days and 6 months post-birth: section 22 *Surrogacy Act 2010* (Qld)[183].

## Which court makes the parentage order?

The Childrens Court of Queensland: section 13 *Surrogacy Act 2010* (Qld)[184]. These applications are ordinarily made in Brisbane, but I have appeared in the Childrens Court (before a District Court level judge, not a magistrate) in Cairns and Townsville.

## Do we have to physically go to court?

Yes, subject to Covid.

## Can the baby go to court?

Yes.

## Can photos be taken in the court?

Ordinarily yes, following representations made by Karen Gough, Kate Cherry and me to the Queensland Law Society to enable that to occur.

## Are the intended parents then the parents for the purposes of Australian law?

Yes: section 60HB *Family Law Act 1975* (Cth), regulation 12CAA *Family Law Regulations 1984* (Cth)- except if the child is born in Victoria- **see chapter 28 interstate arrangements**.

## Have I acted for clients in Queensland about surrogacy?

Yes. My first surrogacy client in Queensland was in 1988. **See chapter 1**.

---

[171] http://www.austlii.edu.au/cgi-bin/viewdoc/au/legis/qld/consol_act/sa2010139/s57.html

[172] http://www.austlii.edu.au/cgi-bin/viewdoc/au/legis/qld/consol_act/sa2010139/s55.html

[173] http://www.austlii.edu.au/cgi-bin/viewdoc/au/legis/qld/consol_act/sa2010139/s54.html

[174] http://www.austlii.edu.au/cgi-bin/viewdoc/au/legis/qld/consol_act/sa2010139/s11.html

[175] http://www.austlii.edu.au/cgi-bin/viewdoc/au/legis/qld/consol_act/sa2010139/s21.html

[176] http://www.austlii.edu.au/cgi-bin/viewdoc/au/legis/qld/consol_act/sa2010139/s22.html

[177] http://www.austlii.edu.au/cgi-bin/viewdoc/au/legis/qld/consol_act/sa2010139/s22.html

[178] http://www.austlii.edu.au/cgi-bin/viewdoc/au/legis/qld/consol_act/sa2010139/s22.html

[179] http://www.austlii.edu.au/cgi-bin/viewdoc/au/legis/qld/consol_act/sa2010139/s22.html

[180] http://www.austlii.edu.au/cgi-bin/viewdoc/au/legis/qld/consol_act/sa2010139/s22.html

[181] RBK v MMJ [2019] QChC 42 http://www.austlii.edu.au/cgi-bin/viewdoc/au/cases/qld/QChC//2019/42.html

[182] http://www8.austlii.edu.au/cgi-bin/viewdoc/au/legis/qld/consol_act/bdamra2003383/s10a.html

[183] http://www.austlii.edu.au/cgi-bin/viewdoc/au/legis/qld/consol_act/sa2010139/s22.html

[184] http://www.austlii.edu.au/cgi-bin/viewdoc/au/legis/qld/consol_act/sa2010139/s13.html

## CHAPTER 24

# SURROGACY IN SOUTH AUSTRALIA

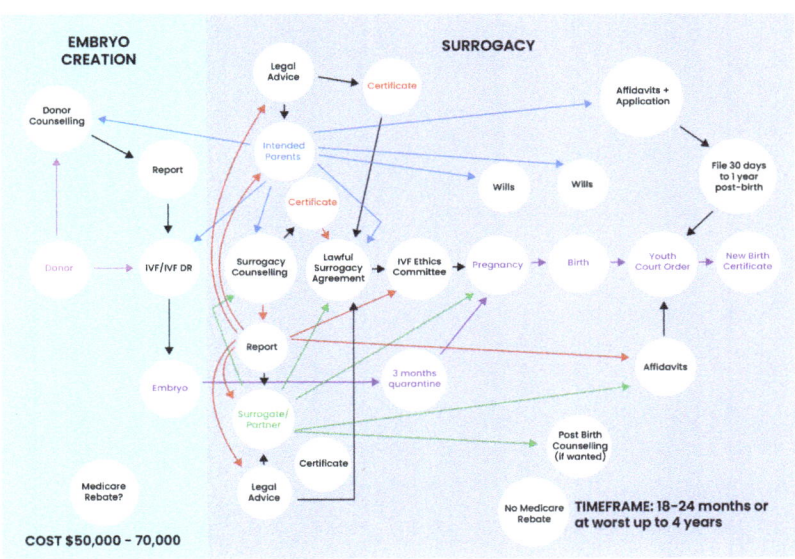

The law governing surrogacy in South Australia is the *Surrogacy Act 2019* (SA) and also the *Assisted Reproductive Treatment Act 1988* (SA).

**Commercial surrogacy**

Section 23 of the *Surrogacy Act 2019*[185] (SA) provides:

*"(1) A person who enters, or purports to enter, a commercial surrogacy agreement is guilty of an offence.*

*Maximum penalty: Imprisonment for 12 months.*

*(2) In proceedings for an offence against this section, the prosecution need not prove that a woman became pregnant, or a child was or is to be born, pursuant to the commercial surrogacy agreement.*

*(3) For the purposes of this section, a reference to a payment will be taken not to include a reference to a payment of reasonable surrogacy costs.*

*(4) In this section—*

*"commercial surrogacy agreement" means a surrogacy agreement that provides for, or purports to provide for, a person to receive payment for any of the following:*

*(a) entering, or agreeing to enter, the surrogacy agreement; or*

*(b) giving up a child, or any rights in respect of a child, born as a result of the surrogacy agreement; or*

*(c) consenting to the making of an order under this Act relating to a child born as a result of the surrogacy arrangement."*

Section 25 of the Surrogacy Act 2019 (SA)[186] provides:

*"(1) A person who, by threat of harm, or by dishonesty or undue influence, induces another to enter a surrogacy agreement is guilty of an offence.*

*Maximum penalty: Imprisonment for 5 years.*

*(2) A person who, for valuable consideration, induces another to enter into a surrogacy agreement is guilty of an offence.*

*Maximum penalty: Imprisonment for 2 years.*

*(3) In proceedings for an offence against this section, the prosecution need not prove that a woman became pregnant, or a child was or is to be born, pursuant to the surrogacy agreement."*

It can be an offence, both in SA and overseas, punishable by up to 15 years imprisonment to pay an egg, sperm or embryo donor a fee. **See chapter 11**.

### Advertising for a surrogate/ advertising seeking intended parents

Section 26 of the *Surrogacy Act 2019* (SA) provides:

*"(1) A person must not publish an advertisement, statement, notice or other material that—*

*(a) seeks, or purports to seek, the agreement of a person to act as a surrogate mother for valuable consideration; or*

*(b) states, or implies, that a person is willing to act as a surrogate mother for valuable consideration.*

*Maximum penalty: $10 000.*

*(2) In proceedings for an offence against this section, it is not necessary for the prosecution to prove that a person did, in fact, as a surrogate mother, or that a surrogacy agreement (whether a lawful surrogacy agreement or otherwise) was, in fact, entered.*

*(3) In this section—*

*"publish" means to disseminate or provide access, by any means, to the public or a section of the public."*

To advertise for an altruistic surrogate is therefore not an offence.

## Where are the offences committed?

In the ACT or anywhere else if the elements of the offence occur in South Australia: section 5G Criminal Law Consolidation Act 1935 (SA)[187]. **See Chapter 11**.

## What should the budget be for surrogacy in SA?

Aim for $70,000. **See chapter 6. See also chapter 2 as to Medicare**.

## How much can a surrogate be paid in South Australia?

She can only be paid her reasonable costs: section 11 *Surrogacy Act 2019* (SA)[188], regulation 5 *Surrogacy Regulations 2020* (SA)[189]. What these are will vary in each case.

## Who can access surrogacy in SA?

Anyone, provided that they are a single or two people: section 10 *Surrogacy Act 2019* (SA)[190]. See chapter 13.

Where can the medical treatment occur?

Anywhere. However, there can be practical limitations to this- so it is best to get legal advice on this first. Clients of mine have obtained parentage orders when medical treatment has occurred interstate or overseas.

The previous law specified ART must occur in SA. I made representations that intended parents should be able to choose where they wanted to undertake IVF. It was good to be listened to.

## Can traditional surrogacy occur?

Yes. It is likely that traditional surrogacy would be handled on a case by case basis by Repromed or Family Fertility Centre.

## Does there need to be a genetic link between the parents and child?

No.

## Must the surrogate already have given birth to another child?

No. Even so, IVF clinics may refuse to provide treatment when the surrogate has not.

## How old do the intended parents have to be to enter into the surrogacy arrangement?

25 or older: section 10 *Surrogacy Act 2010* (SA)[191].

## How old do the surrogate and her partner have to be to enter into the surrogacy arrangement?

The surrogate has to be 25 or older: section 10 *Surrogacy Act 2019* (SA)[192]. Oddly, there is no age specified for her partner. While in theory someone under 18 could enter into a surrogacy arrangement, under the *Family Law Act* 1975 (Cth) that person's parents absent a court order have parental responsibility, then it is clear that the surrogate and her partner have to be 18 or older. It is unclear whether the surrogate's partner can be a party to a lawful surrogacy agreement, although the partner is a parent under the *Family Relationships Act 1975* (SA) and possibly the *Family Law Act 1975* (Cth) so his or her consent to the process would ordinarily be considered necessary.

## Does the surrogacy arrangement need to be written?

Yes, and must be in a certain form: section 10 *Surrogacy Act 2019* (SA)[193].

## Does independent legal advice have to be provided before entering into the surrogacy arrangement?

Yes: section 10 *Surrogacy Act 2019* (SA)[194].

## Does counselling need to be obtained before the surrogacy arrangement is entered into?

Yes: sections 10, 14 *Surrogacy Act 2019* (SA)[195] [196]. There are requirements about how counselling is undertaken and by whom.

## Who are the parents when the child is born?

The surrogate and her partner: section 8 *Surrogacy Act 2019* (SA), *Family Relationships Act 1975* (SA).

## Who are named on the birth certificate as the parents?

The surrogate and her partner: *Family Relationships Act 1975* (SA).

## Is a post-birth report or counselling required?

No. However, the surrogate can insist on having counselling through the pregnancy and after, at the cost of the intended parents: section 15 *Surrogacy Act 2019* (SA), This provision arose due to a case in which I acted for the surrogate and her husband. I made representations to ensure that in future surrogates could have access to counselling if needed.

## When can the application be made to the Court for a parentage order?

Only between when the baby is 30 days and 12 months old: section 18 *Surrogacy Act 2019* (SA)[197].

## Which court makes the parentage order?

The Youth Court of SA: section 4 *Surrogacy Act 2019* (SA).

## Do we have to physically go to court?

Yes, subject to Covid.

## Can the baby go to court?

Yes.

## Can photos be taken in the court?

Check with the court.

**Are the intended parents then the parents for the purposes of Australian law?**

Yes: section 60HB *Family Law Act 1975* (Cth), regulation 12CAA *Family Law Regulations 1984* (Cth)- except if the child is born in Victoria- **see chapter 28 interstate arrangements**.

**Have I acted for clients in South Australia about surrogacy?**

Yes. My first surrogacy clients in South Australia were in about 2012.

---

[185] http://www.austlii.edu.au/cgi-bin/viewdoc/au/legis/sa/consol_act/sa2019139/s23.html

[186] http://www.austlii.edu.au/cgi-bin/viewdoc/au/legis/sa/consol_act/sa2019139/s25.html

[187] http://www.austlii8.edu.au/cgi-bin/viewdoc/au/legis/sa/consol_act/clca1935262/s5g.html

[188] http://www.austlii.edu.au/cgi-bin/viewdoc/au/legis/sa/consol_act/sa2019139/s11.html

[189] http://www.austlii.edu.au/cgi-bin/viewdoc/au/legis/sa/consol_reg/sr2020248/s5.html

[190] http://www.austlii.edu.au/cgi-bin/viewdoc/au/legis/sa/consol_act/sa2019139/s10.html

[191] http://www.austlii.edu.au/cgi-bin/viewdoc/au/legis/sa/consol_act/sa2019139/s10.html

[192] http://www.austlii.edu.au/cgi-bin/viewdoc/au/legis/sa/consol_act/sa2019139/s10.html

[193] http://www.austlii.edu.au/cgi-bin/viewdoc/au/legis/sa/consol_act/sa2019139/s10.html

[194] http://www.austlii.edu.au/cgi-bin/viewdoc/au/legis/sa/consol_act/sa2019139/s10.html

[195] http://www.austlii.edu.au/cgi-bin/viewdoc/au/legis/sa/consol_act/sa2019139/s10.html

[196] http://www.austlii.edu.au/cgi-bin/viewdoc/au/legis/sa/consol_act/sa2019139/s14.html

[197] http://www.austlii.edu.au/cgi-bin/viewdoc/au/legis/sa/consol_act/sa2019139/s18.html

## CHAPTER 25

# SURROGACY IN TASMANIA

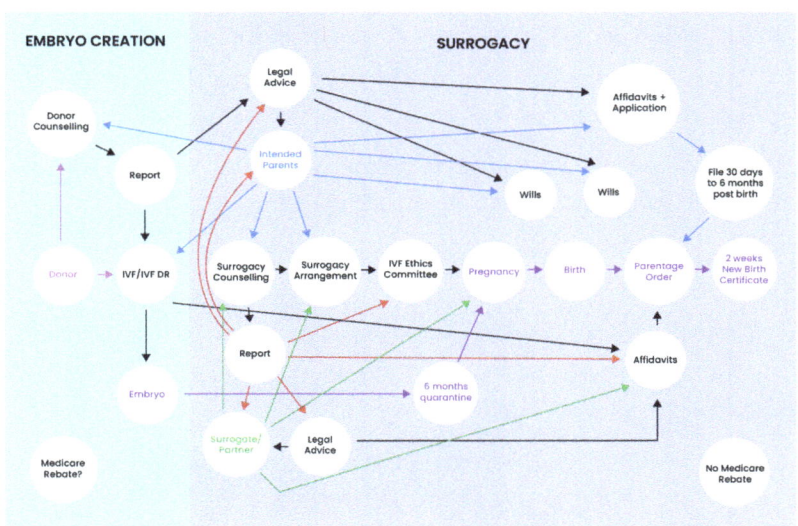

COST $50,000-70,000          TIMEFRAME: 18-24 months or at worst up to 4 years

Surrogacy in Tasmania is governed by the *Surrogacy Act 2012* (Tas).

**Commercial surrogacy**

Section 40 of the *Surrogacy Act 2012* (Tas) provides:

*"A person must not enter into, or offer to enter into, a commercial surrogacy arrangement.*

*Penalty: Fine not exceeding 100 penalty units."*

It can be an offence, both in the ACT and overseas, punishable by up to 15 years imprisonment to pay an egg, sperm or embryo donor a fee. **See chapter 11**.

**Advertising for a surrogate/ advertising seeking intended parents**

Section 41 of the *Surrogacy Act 2012* (Tas)[198] provides:

*"(1) In this section –*

***payment*** *means –*

189

*(a) payment in money or money's worth, other than payment of the birth mother's reasonable surrogacy costs; and*

*(b) for reward or other material benefit or advantage, other than payment of any of the birth mother's reasonable surrogacy costs.*

*(2) A person must not, for payment, or in anticipation of receiving payment –*

*(a) initiate or take part in any negotiations with a view to the making of a surrogacy arrangement; or*

*(b) offer or agree to negotiate the making of a surrogacy arrangement; or*

*(c) compile any information with a view to its use in making, or negotiating the making of, any surrogacy arrangements; or*

*(d) knowingly cause another person to do any of the acts referred to in paragraph (a), (b) or (c) .*

*Penalty: Fine not exceeding 100 penalty units."*

Decoded, provided it is an altruistic surrogacy arrangement you can advertise for a surrogate.

## Where are the offences committed?

Only in Tasmania.

## What should the budget be for surrogacy in Tasmania?

Aim for $70,000. **See chapter 6. See also chapter 2 as to Medicare**.

## How much can a surrogate be paid in Tasmania?

She can only be paid her reasonable costs: section 9 *Surrogacy Act 2019* (Tas)[199]. What these are will vary in each case.

## Who can access surrogacy in Tasmania?

Anyone, provided that everyone lives in Tasmania: section 16 Surrogacy Act 2012 (Tas)[200]. **See chapter 13**.

## Where can the medical treatment occur?

Anywhere. However, there can be practical limitations to this- so it is best to get legal advice on this first.

## Can traditional surrogacy occur?

Yes: section 23 *Surrogacy Act 2012* (Tas)[201]. However, it is unlikely that either of the clinics, Genea or TasIVF, will undertake traditional surrogacy.

## Does there need to be a genetic link between the parents and child?

No.

## Must the surrogate already have given birth to another child?

Yes: section 16 *Surrogacy Act 2012* (Tas)[202].

## How old do the intended parents have to be to enter into the surrogacy arrangement?

21 or older: section 16 Surrogacy Act 2012 (Tas)[203].

## How old do the surrogate and her partner have to be to enter into the surrogacy arrangement?

The surrogate has to be 25 or older: section 16 *Surrogacy Act 2012* (Tas)[204]. Oddly, there is no age specified for her partner. While in theory someone under 18 could enter into a surrogacy arrangement, under the *Family Law Act 1975* (Cth) that person's parents absent a court order have parental responsibility, then it is clear that the surrogate and her partner have to be 18 or older. It is unclear whether the surrogate's partner can be a party to a lawful surrogacy agreement, although the partner is a parent under the *Status of Children Act 1974* (Tas) and possibly the *Family Law Act 1975* (Cth) so his or her consent to the process would ordinarily be considered necessary.

## Does the surrogacy arrangement need to be written?

Yes: section 16 Surrogacy Act 2012 (Tas)[205].

## Does independent legal advice have to be provided before entering into the surrogacy arrangement?

Yes: section 16 Surrogacy Act 2012 (Tas)[206].

## Does counselling need to be obtained before the surrogacy arrangement is entered into?

Yes: section 16 Surrogacy Act 2012 (Tas)[207].

## Who are the parents when the child is born?
The surrogate and her partner: *Status of Children Act 1974* (Tas).

## Who are named on the birth certificate as the parents?
The surrogate and her partner: *Status of Children Act 1974* (Tas).

## Is a post-birth report or counselling required?
No.

## When can the application be made to the Court for a parentage order?
Ordinarily between when the baby is 30 days and 6 months old: section 15 *Surrogacy Act 2012* (Tas)[208].

## Which court makes the parentage order?
Magistrates Court (Children's Division): section 4 *Surrogacy Act 2012* (Tas).

## Do we have to physically go to court?
Check with the court.

## Can the baby go to court?
Check with the court.

## Can photos be taken in the court?
Check with the court.

## Are the intended parents then the parents for the purposes of Australian law?
Yes: section 60HB *Family Law Act 1975* (Cth), regulation 12CAA *Family Law Regulations 1984* (Cth)- except if the child is born in Victoria- *see chapter 28 interstate arrangements.*

## Have I acted for clients in Tasmania about surrogacy?
Yes. My first surrogacy clients in Tasmania were in about 2011.

[198]

[199] http://www.austlii.edu.au/cgi-bin/viewdoc/au/legis/tas/consol_act/sa2012139/s9.html

[200] http://www.austlii.edu.au/cgi-bin/viewdoc/au/legis/tas/consol_act/sa2012139/s16.html

[201] http://www.austlii.edu.au/cgi-bin/viewdoc/au/legis/tas/consol_act/sa2012139/s23.html

[202] http://www.austlii.edu.au/cgi-bin/viewdoc/au/legis/tas/consol_act/sa2012139/s16.html

[203] http://www.austlii.edu.au/cgi-bin/viewdoc/au/legis/tas/consol_act/sa2012139/s16.html

[204] http://www.austlii.edu.au/cgi-bin/viewdoc/au/legis/tas/consol_act/sa2012139/s16.html

[205] http://www.austlii.edu.au/cgi-bin/viewdoc/au/legis/tas/consol_act/sa2012139/s16.html

[206] http://www.austlii.edu.au/cgi-bin/viewdoc/au/legis/tas/consol_act/sa2012139/s16.html

[207] http://www.austlii.edu.au/cgi-bin/viewdoc/au/legis/tas/consol_act/sa2012139/s16.html

[208] http://www.austlii.edu.au/cgi-bin/viewdoc/au/legis/tas/consol_act/sa2012139/s15.html

CHAPTER 26

# SURROGACY IN VICTORIA

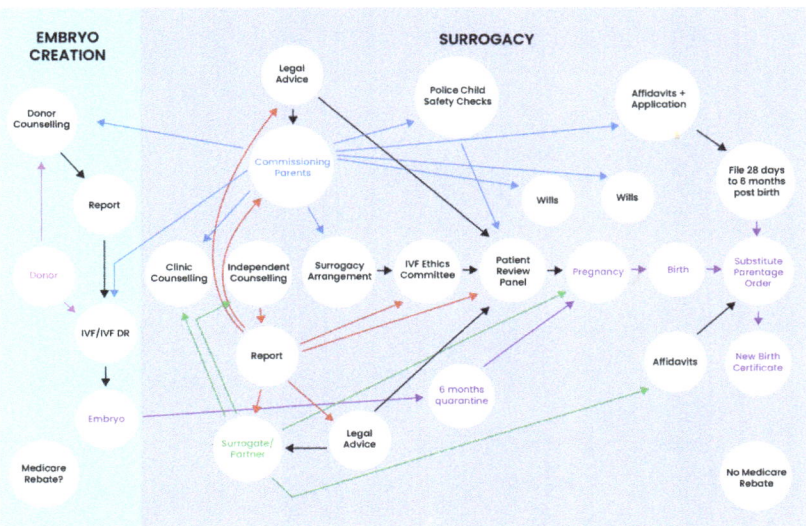

Surrogacy in Victoria is regulated by the *Assisted Reproductive Treatment Act 2008* (Vic)[209], the *Assisted Reproductive Treatment Regulations 2019* (Vic)[210] and the *Status of Children Act 1974* (Vic)[211]. Traditional surrogacy cannot be undertaken through an IVF clinic. Gestational surrogacy applications through IVF clinics must be made to the State regulator, the Patient Review Panel before treatment can commence. Victoria, Western Australia, New Zealand and Israel are the only places in the world that require State sanction before intended parents can proceed with surrogacy. The irony about such a proscriptive process in Victoria is that there are virtually no protections when there is a traditional surrogacy arrangement, unlike other States.

195

# Applications for approval of surrogacy arrangements to the Patient Review Panel 2010-2019

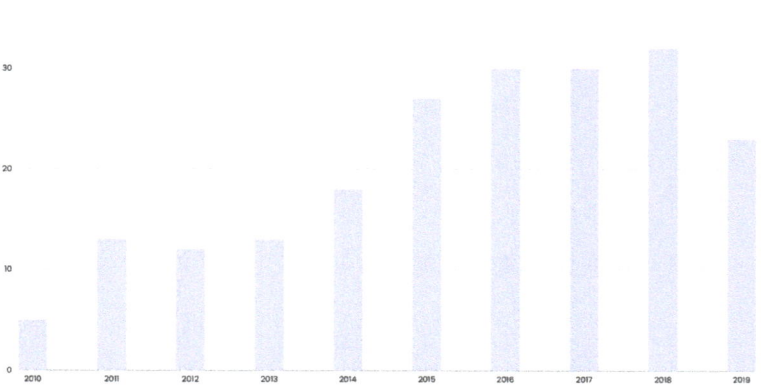

The Patient Review Panel has set out at length its requirements for approval, in a Guidance Note:

> *"A registered ART provider may carry out treatment under a surrogacy arrangement only if the arrangement has been approved by the Panel (section 39 of the ART Act).*
>
> *The Panel may approve a surrogacy arrangement if it is satisfied of the following matters set out in section 40 of the ART Act:*
>
> a. *that a doctor has formed an opinion that the commissioning parent is unlikely to become pregnant, be able to carry a pregnancy or give birth; or, if the commissioning parent is a woman, the woman is likely to place her life or health, or that of the baby, at risk if she becomes pregnant, carries a pregnancy or gives birth.*
> b. *that the surrogate mother's oocyte will not be used in the conception of the child.*
> c. *that the surrogate mother has previously carried a pregnancy and given birth to a live child.*
> d. *that the surrogate mother is at least 25 years of age.*

e. *that the commissioning parent/s, the surrogate mother and the surrogate mother's partner (if any) have received counselling and legal advice as required under section 43 of the ART Act, which requires that they have:*
   i. *undergone counselling, by a counsellor providing services on behalf of a registered ART provider, about the social and psychological implications of entering into the arrangement, including counselling about the 'prescribed matters';*
   ii. *undergone counselling about the implications of the relinquishment of the child and the relationship between the surrogate mother and the child once it is born; and,*
   iii. *obtained information about the legal consequences of entering into the arrangement.*
f. *that the parties to the surrogacy arrangement are aware of and understand the personal and legal consequences of the arrangement.*
g. *that the parties to the surrogacy arrangement are prepared for the consequences if the arrangement does not proceed in accordance with the parties' intentions, including the consequences if the commissioning parent/s decides not to accept the child once born; and the consequences if the surrogate mother refuses to relinquish the child to the commissioning parent/s.*
h. *that the parties to the surrogacy arrangement are able to make informed decisions about proceeding with the arrangement.*

Section 40(2)(a) of the ART Act also requires the Panel to have regard to a report from a counsellor providing services on behalf of a registered ART provider.

In carrying out its functions, the Panel is also required to give effect to the guiding principles of the ART Act, set out in Section 5, that are:

a. *the welfare and interests of persons born or to be born as a result of treatment procedures are paramount;*

b. *at no time should the use of treatment procedures be for the purpose of exploiting, in trade or otherwise the reproductive capabilities of men and women or children born as a result of treatment procedures;*
c. *children born as the result of the use of donated gametes have a right to information about their genetic parents;*
d. *the health and wellbeing of persons undergoing treatment procedures must be protected at all times;*
e. *persons seeking to undergo treatment procedures must not be discriminated against on the basis of their sexual orientation, marital status, race or religion.*

1. *What documents are needed to make an application to the Panel?*

*The **mandatory documents** that must be provided to the Panel are:*

a. *a surrogacy arrangement application form, signed and dated by all parties, including by any donor and their partners;*
b. *a report from a counsellor providing services on behalf of a registered ART provider that addresses the prescribed matters;*
c. *proof of the surrogate mother's age (for example, a certified copy of a passport, driver licence or birth certificate);*
d. *proof that the surrogate mother has given birth to a live child (for example, a certified copy of a birth certificate);*
e. *subject to the exceptions mentioned at point 4 below, a letter from a doctor confirming that the commissioning parent is unlikely to become pregnant, be able to carry a pregnancy or give birth, or if the commissioning parent is a woman that the woman is likely to place her life or health, or that of the baby, at risk if she becomes pregnant, carries a pregnancy or gives birth;*
f. *a report or memorandum of the legal advice provided to the commissioning parent/s; and,*

g. *a report or memorandum of the legal advice provided to the surrogate and her partner (if any).*

The **additional documents** *that the Panel also requests, but which are not mandatory to provide, are:*

a. *a report prepared by an independent psychologist[212] who has assessed the commissioning parent/s and surrogate mother and her partner (if any);*
b. *a letter from a doctor or other medical professional discussing the surrogate mother's health and suitability, and outlining any risks that have been discussed with her;*
c. *a letter from a doctor or other medical professional discussing the commissioning parent/s physical or mental health (only where one or both of the commissioning parents have a chronic illness, disability or other serious health condition);*
d. *Victorian Assisted Reproductive Treatment Authority (VARTA) approval for the import of embryos (only where interstate embryos formed from donor gametes are to be used in the proposed arrangement);*
e. *a signed copy of a surrogacy agreement (only where the applicants have made one);*
f. *copies of any consent forms signed by applicants, including gamete donors, that indicates their informed consent to treatment.*

*Where there are matters raised in the application documentation which the Panel considers relevant to its consideration of the application and to giving effect to the guiding principles of the ART Act, the Panel may request other material on a case-by-case basis. This will be communicated to the applicants and/or their ART clinics as soon as practicable after receipt of the application.*

*For example, the Panel may request a party or parties to a surrogacy arrangement to provide a copy of a National Police Certificate or seek their consent to obtain child protection records if relevant matters of this nature are in issue. Where serious offences are disclosed, either in the application paperwork generally or following a request by the Panel for a criminal record check, the Panel may request additional documentation such as court files and/or reports. Similarly, where an application indicates that an applicant has a serious physical or mental health issue, the Panel may ask for medical records and/or further information from the applicant's treating specialist to assist it in understanding the condition and the impact on the applicant in the context of a surrogacy arrangement.*

*While it is not mandatory to provide the additional documents listed above, the Panel is greatly assisted by them and, if they are not provided, the Panel may determine that it does not have enough information to be able to properly consider the application. This can lead to delays while the Panel seeks additional information that it considers it needs in order to be satisfied of the legislative requirements, or it can result in an application not being approved.*

*4.1 Counselling report*

*The prescribed matters that must be covered in the mandatory counselling are listed in regulation 10 of the Assisted Reproductive Treatment Regulations 2019 (the Regulations) and are:*

a. *the implications of surrogacy for the relationship between:*
   - *all parties to the surrogacy arrangement including the commissioning parent/s; and*
   - *if the surrogate mother has a partner, the surrogate mother and her partner; and*
   - *the commissioning parent/s and the surrogate mother; and*
   - *if donor gametes or embryos are to be used, the donor and the donor's partner, if any, and all parties to the surrogacy.*
b. *the implications of surrogacy for any existing children of the surrogate mother or the commissioning parent/s.*
c. *the possibility of medical complications for the surrogate mother or the child.*

d. *the possibility of any party deciding not to proceed with the surrogacy.*
e. *the attitudes of all parties towards the conduct of the pregnancy.*
f. *the attitudes of all parties to investigation of a genetic abnormality, the possibility of termination of pregnancy or other complications.*
g. *the need for the parties to agree on a process for resolving disputes relating to the pregnancy; or arising during the pregnancy.*
h. *if there are 2 commissioning parents, the commissioning parents' intentions for care of the child if one of them dies.*
i. *possible grief reactions on the part of the surrogate mother and her partner, if any.*
j. *ways of telling the child about surrogacy;*
k. *attitudes toward an ongoing relationship between the surrogate mother, her family and the child.*

*Clinic counsellors who are preparing a report for the Panel should note that it is important to provide a detailed explanation of what was discussed and agreed upon by the relevant parties rather than just stating that what issues were discussed.*

*If, upon review, Panel staff determine that one of the prescribed matters has not been covered in the counselling report or that the Panel would be assisted by more details regarding one or more of the prescribed matters then clinic counsellors may be requested to provide an amended or addendum report.*

*The Panel is also greatly assisted when counselling reports also address the following matters which are not listed in the Regulations:*

a. *general information about the history of the relationships between all of the parties, including when and how they met, how long any couples who are parties to the arrangement have been in a relationship and lived together, and the genders and ages of any existing children of any party to the arrangement;*

b. *the surrogate mother's motivation for offering to act as a surrogate, including whether she would consider acting as a surrogate for anyone else or just the commissioning parents;*
c. *specific details of any support network/s available to the surrogate that can provide emotional, psychological and practical support during and after a pregnancy, including friends, family and professional support services, if applicable;*
d. *the attitudes of all parties to a multiple birth;*
e. *the intentions of the parties should a child be born with a serious medical condition or disability;*
f. *if there is 1 commissioning parent, their intentions for the care of the child if they were to die;*
g. *if there are 2 commissioning parents, their intentions for the care of the child if both of them were to die;*
h. *how the surrogacy arrangement will be discussed with the existing children of all parties (if any);*
i. *any agreement about lifestyle factors for the surrogate mother during the pregnancy, such as consumption of alcohol, smoking, diet or exercise;*
j. *where the birth is to take place and what plans have been made regarding how and when the relinquishment of the baby will occur;*
k. *the attitudes of the parties to any relevant religious or cultural practices (e.g. circumcision); and*
l. *any agreement that the parties have made in relation to medical decisions, such as vaccinations, for the child in the period of time up until a Substitute Parentage Order is made.*

### Donor gametes

*Where donor gametes or embryos are proposed to be used in the arrangement, the Panel is greatly assisted by information in the counsellor's report about:*
a. *if the commissioning parents are in a same-sex relationship and one of them is using their own gametes to form an embryo, what agreement has been made*

*regarding which commissioning parents' gametes will be used;*

b. *the donor's background and relationship to the commissioning parent/s;*
c. *the donor's motivation for offering to donate their gametes and whether they would consider being a donor for anyone else or just the commissioning parents;*
d. *all the parties' understanding of the requirements of the ART Act in relation to disclosing the identity of the donor to any child born;*
e. *implications of using the proposed donor for the surrogate and her partner if any;*
f. *the implications of the arrangement for the donor, including expectations about future relationship with the recipient/s, impacts on the relationship with the recipient(s) if the donation/pregnancy is not successful and how they would feel if the arrangement did not proceed as intended (e.g. issues with relinquishment);*
g. *ways of telling a child born that they are donor conceived;*
h. *the possible impact of the arrangement on the donor's children if any.*

*Counsellors are encouraged to explore any other issues in the report that they feel are relevant to the application.*

### *Format of Report*

*The Panel is greatly assisted by counselling reports that comprehensively address each prescribed matter under its own separate heading and, preferably, in the order listed in the Regulations.*

*Counselling reports should be provided on clinic letterhead, provide the name, contact details and signature of the counsellor/s who provided the counselling and/ or authored the report and should include numbered paragraphs and numbered pages for ease of reference.*

*Clinic counsellors should ensure that all parties to the arrangement are provided with, and have read, the counselling report before making an application to the Panel.*

**Manner of counselling**

*While Panel understands that it is not always possible to conduct all counselling in face-to-face sessions, it has a preference that the parties to the arrangement have received at least one face-to-face session each and one face-to-face group session, where clinic policies, public health advice and the advice of relevant professional associations designed to limit the spread of COVID-19 allow. Where such policies and advice dictate that face-to face counselling should not occur, the Panel will continue to support the use of Zoom, Skype, Teams or equivalent videoconferencing for individual and group counselling sessions by ART counsellors Where internet access is not available, counselling conducted by teleconferencing is acceptable.*

*Counsellors should clearly state on their written reports where video/teleconferencing facilities have been used and any perceived limitations in the accuracy of the assessment as a result of this.*

*Where a clinic has moved to non-face-to-face counselling, and where an applicant specifically requests a face-to-face session rather than videoconference for any reason, the clinic should consider this in line with its own occupational health and safety policies and any applicable professional and Victorian or Federal government guidelines issued at the relevant time.*

*Where a clinic has returned to face-to-face counselling, and where an applicant specifically requests a video-conference session instead for any reason, the clinic should consider its own policies, and the individual clinical needs of the applicant in deciding whether to agree to this. It will be helpful for the Panel in such a case for this is explained in the counselling report.*

*4.2 Letter from a doctor/medical professional regarding the commissioning parent/s*

*In order to be able to approve an application, the ART Act requires that the Panel to be satisfied that that a doctor has formed an opinion that, in the circumstances, the commissioning parent is unlikely to become pregnant, be able to carry a pregnancy, or give birth; or if the commissioning parent is a woman, the woman is likely to place her life or health, or that of the baby, at risk if she becomes pregnant, carries a pregnancy or gives birth. As such, the Panel requires a letter from a doctor confirming this. It is important that any medical letter that is provided clearly and explicitly states why the surrogacy arrangement is required and not just that the author supports the proposed surrogacy arrangement.*

*Despite the preceding paragraph, the Panel does not require applicants to provide a letter from a doctor confirming that the commissioning parent is unlikely to become pregnant, be able to carry a pregnancy, or give birth in the following circumstances where there is no female commissioning parent:*

a. *same-sex male commissioning parents; or*
b. *single male commissioning parent.*[213]

*Where a commissioning parent has been diagnosed with a chronic illness, disability or other serious health condition, the Panel asks that this is addressed in a letter from the relevant treating medical professional. This letter should outline the severity and impact of the illness or condition and its current treatment and prognosis.*

*While it is one factor that the Panel will take into consideration when making its decision, applicants and clinics should note that the fact that a commissioning parent has such an illness or condition is not a barrier in and of itself to their application being considered or approved by the Panel.*

*4.3 Letter from a doctor/medical professional regarding the surrogate mother*

*The Panel asks that a letter be provided from a doctor or other relevant medical professional that discusses the surrogate mother's health and suitability to carry a pregnancy, and outlines any risks that have been discussed with her.*

*In individual cases, the Panel may request an additional medical letter or report for a surrogate mother if they:*

a. *are of an advanced maternal age;*
b. *have a complex obstetric history, including but not limited to:*
   i. *post-partum haemorrhage;*
   ii. *miscarriage;*
   iii. *emergency hysterectomy; and/or*
   iv. *gestational diabetes;*
c. *have a history of mental health issues, including but not limited to perinatal anxiety and/or depression.*

*Where a surrogate mother is currently prescribed a medication that may have implications for a pregnancy (for example, contraindicated due to a risk of birth defects) then this should also be addressed in the doctor's letter including what, if any, impact ceasing the medication during a pregnancy may have on the surrogate mother's health.*

*Commissioning parent/s and surrogate mothers who are unsure whether their age, a health condition or medication that they are currently taking would be of relevance to their surrogacy application should consult with their ART provider or other relevant health professional before making an application to the Panel.*

*4.4 Psychological assessment*

*Undergoing an independent psychological assessment and having the psychologist provide a report to the Panel is not mandatory. However, in order to approve an application, the Panel must be satisfied that parties are aware of and understand the personal consequences of entering into the proposed arrangement and are making informed decisions. To achieve this, the Panel is often greatly assisted by an independent psychological assessment report.*

*The independent psychologist's report is intended to provide a view of the applicants that is independent of the applicants' view of themselves and independent of the view provided by the applicants' ART clinic and reflected in the counselling report. Therefore, for a psychological assessment to be independent, the assessing psychologist should not be an employee of an ART clinic in Victoria, not be receiving payment for services provided to an ART clinic and not have a direct or indirect financial or personal interest in an ART clinic.*

*Any independent assessment should not duplicate the prescribed counselling requirements and should focus on:*

a. *the applicants' individual psychological preparedness for the arrangement;*
b. *the implications of the arrangement for the applicants including respective partners and any existing children;*
c. *the applicants' ability to provide informed consent to the arrangement;*
d. *any concerns about the applicants' psychopathology that may impact upon the arrangement.*

*Where applicants have a history of mental health issues and are currently receiving treatment from a psychiatrist, psychologist, therapist or other relevant mental health professional, the Panel may request a report from that treating professional that also focusses on the matters outlined above. The Panel would also be assisted if the author of the independent psychological assessment report consults with that mental health professional prior to the drafting of the report to ensure that all relevant issues are covered.*

*As with counselling, the Panel prefers that psychological assessments be conducted in person. However, in light of the COVID-19 pandemic, and having consulted the field, the Panel supports the decision of individual psychologists to use Zoom, Skype or equivalent videoconferencing for individual counselling sessions where they think this is appropriate, following practice policies and the advice of professional associations, and while social distancing is required to manage the COVID-19 situation. Where internet access is not available, counselling conducted by teleconferencing is acceptable. Where the psychologist undertaking an assessment has resumed seeing clients face-to-face, then the assessment for the Panel would preferably also be conducted face-to-face, but the Panel leaves this to the assessing psychologist to determine in consultation with the applicant.*

*Psychologists should state clearly on their written reports where video/teleconferencing facilities have been used and any perceived limitations in the accuracy of the assessment as a result of this.*

*4.5 Legal advice*

*As it is a requirement that the Panel be satisfied that the parties to the arrangement understand the legal consequences of the arrangement and that they are prepared for the consequences if the arrangement does not proceed in accordance with their intentions, the Panel asks that the commissioning parent/s and the surrogate mother and her partner (if any) provide the Panel with a written memorandum or report of the legal advice has been provided to them.*

*Legal advice may be provided face-to-face or via videoconferencing, where possible, during the COVID-19 pandemic.*

*To avoid the potential of a conflict of interest, applicants should ensure that the commissioning parent/s and the surrogate mother and her partner (if any) have received legal advice from different lawyers and that those lawyers are not parties to the arrangement.*

*At a minimum, the legal advice should cover the following matters:*

*a. the legal status of the child at the time of birth;*
*b. the consequences if the commissioning parents refuse or are unable to accept the child once it is born;*

c. *the consequences if the surrogate refuses to relinquish the child once it is born or refuses to consent to the making of the Substitute Parentage Order;*
d. *the need and process for the commissioning parents to apply to the court for a Substitute Parentage Order, including the relevant time-frames for making the application;*
e. *arrangements for the care of the child prior to the making of a Substitute Parentage Order; and*
f. *arrangements for giving consent to medical treatment for the child prior to the making of a Substitute Parentage Order; and*
g. *the requirement that the arrangement be altruistic and the prescribed costs that may be reimbursed.*

*Where one or more of the applicants live interstate or in another country, the legal advice should also address:*

a. *where it intended that the child be born;*
b. *the implications of the child being born in a jurisdiction other than Victoria (interstate or overseas), including the legal status of the child, its parentage, and matters such as registering the birth and liaison with the Victorian Registrar of Births, Deaths and Marriages.*

*Legal practitioners are encouraged to address any substantial differences between the relevant jurisdiction's legislation as it may affect the process of obtaining a Substitute Parentage Order (if applicable) and make reference to any enquiries the practitioner has made with the relevant jurisdiction's equivalent of the Registrar of Births, Deaths and Marriages regarding their processes for managing the registration of Victorian Substitute Parentage Orders.*

*Where **donor gametes/embryos** are intended to be used in the proposed arrangement, the legal advice should also address:*

- the right of the donor to withdraw consent to the treatment procedure at any time before embryo transfer and any associated implications;

- the rights of donor-conceived children to identifying and non-identifying information about their donor/s;
- the information that is held on the Central Register and the Voluntary Register, including who can access what types of information about the arrangement, including information about the donor and other parties to the arrangement, and the process for accessing that information.

*The legal advice should be fully up-to-date and reflect the law at the time the advice is being given. This should include any recent changes to the law, such as the changes to what a surrogate may be lawfully reimbursed for under the Assisted Reproductive Treatment Regulations 2019 which commenced on 13 December 2019. If, upon review by Panel staff or the Panel Chairperson, it appears that any legal advice provided to any of the parties to the arrangement is out of date, inaccurate or incomplete then the application will not be able to be listed for hearing until further legal advice has been sought by the affected parties and a summary of that advice provided to the Panel.*

*4.6 Surrogacy agreements*

*Surrogacy agreements are not required in Victoria in order to enter into a surrogacy arrangement and are not enforceable other than in relation to the reimbursement of the prescribed costs actually incurred by the surrogate. However, if applicants have made a written agreement, it would greatly assist the Panel to be provided with a signed and dated copy."*

*The Guidance Note then goes on to say how the Patient Review Panel hears applications:*

*"Upon receipt of an application, it will be reviewed by Panel staff and/or the Panel Chairperson. Applicants and/or clinic staff will be advised if any missing/additional information is required or requested.*

***Applications will only be listed for hearing once they are complete and all documentation has been provided. Applications are not considered to be complete until***

*missing or requested additional information has been received. If applications are incomplete but applicants insist on being listed for hearing, then the matter will be referred by Panel staff to the Panel Chairperson for review prior to listing for hearing.*

Once a hearing date has been allocated, applicants will receive a Notice of Hearing stating:

a. the nature of the hearing; and
b. the time and place of the hearing; and
c. that the applicant is entitled to be present at the hearing, to make submissions and to be accompanied by another person; and
d. that the hearing is not open to the public; and
e. that there is no right to legal representation at the hearing without leave from the Panel; and
f. the possible findings or orders that the Panel may make.

**It is the preference of the Panel that all parties to a surrogacy arrangement, including donors and their partners (if any), attend the Panel hearing, either in person or via videoconference.**

If one or more party to an arrangement is unable to attend a Panel hearing in person, then it may be possible for them to participate in the hearing via telephone. This request should be made in writing to the Panel and will be considered on a case-by-case basis by the Panel Chairperson.

Applicants asking to participate in the hearing via telephone should be aware that the Panel may adjourn or even not approve the application if it cannot satisfy itself of its legislative requirements by speaking to one or more applicants on the telephone rather than in person.

When face-to-face Panel hearings are convened, they are held at the Department of Health Head Office located at **50 Lonsdale Street, Melbourne, Victoria, 3000** unless otherwise advised. Upon arriving at 50 Lonsdale Street, applicants will need to pick up a security pass from the *ground floor reception and make their way up to the level where the hearing is being held.*

*Every level has a foyer area with chairs and applicants should use their passes to enter the foyer and take a seat until they are invited into the hearing room by either one of the Panel members or a Panel staff member.*

*Panel hearings consist of a division of five Panel members including the Chairperson, a Deputy Chairperson and three other Panel members, at least one of whom will be an expect in child protection matters. Up to three Panel staff members may also be in attendance to take notes and/or provide legal advice to the Panel members.*

*Panel hearings generally last for up to an hour (or longer if required) and towards the end of the hearing applicants will be asked to leave the room for a short period of time to allow the members to discuss the application. At times, the Panel may also request to speak to one or more of the parties to the arrangement alone.*

*In some circumstances, the Chairperson may decide that an application is suitable to be considered on the papers and without the applicants having to attend a Panel hearing. This is, however, determined on a case-by-case basis and is at the discretion of the Chairperson of the Panel. In that case, applicants are still entitled to attend the hearing of their application should they wish to.*

> **IMPORTANT NOTE:**
>
> *In light of the COVID-19 pandemic, the Panel will conduct all hearings by videoconference using Microsoft Teams from April 2020 until further notice.*
>
> *Comprehensive instructions to assist applicants to participate in hearings conducted by videoconference will be provided together with the Notice of Hearing.*
>
> *Applicants who are unable to participate in a hearing by videoconference are advised to communicate with Panel staff as soon as possible upon receipt of the Notice of Hearing to formally request an alternative method of participating in the hearing (such as attending via teleconference, subject to the approval of the Panel Chairperson).*

7. What does the Panel consider when making its decision?

The Panel must have regard to the specific sections in Part 4 of the Act, and what it must be satisfied of, the legislative context, including the purpose of the Act (to regulate assisted reproductive treatment in Victoria) and the guiding principles set out in section 5 of the Act[214].

It must be satisfied of all the matters set out in section and summarised above in section 3 of this guidance note (pages 5-6), unless it determines that it will approve a non-complying arrangement under section 41 (see section 5 above of the guidance not) and must have regard to the guiding principles of the Act.

If there is a conflict between the welfare and interests of the child to be born, and the health and wellbeing of the applicants, any conflict must be resolved in favour of the child's welfare and interests[215].

8. The Panel's decision

8.1 Possible outcomes of a Panel decision

The possible decisions that the Panel may make are:

a. *that the surrogacy arrangement is approved;*
b. *that the surrogacy arrangement is not approved;*
c. *that that the surrogacy arrangement is approved subject to any conditions imposed by the Panel.*

*8.2 Notification of the Panel's decision*

*Where possible, the Panel will advise applicants whether the surrogacy arrangement has been approved or not via email or telephone communication by Panel staff on either the day of the hearing or the following day. At times, it will require more time to consider the application or may require more information before it makes its decision.*

*If the Panel does not consider that it can make a decision within 1-2 days of the hearing then it will advise applicants within that time frame and advise them of what will happen next.*

*8.3 Certificate*

*Once the Panel has made a decision, applicants will be provided with a certificate stating the decision within 14 days of the hearing or, if the hearing has been adjourned, within 14 days of the date that the decision was made. An electronic copy of this certificate will also be provided to the relevant ART clinic for their records.*

*Under section 91(3) of the ART Act, the Panel may impose any conditions it considers necessary and reasonable in the circumstances of the decision and, if the Panel chooses to place a condition on its decision, it will be stated on the certificate.*

*8.4 Reasons for decision*

*The Panel is also required by the ART Act to provide applicants with written reasons for its decision. These reasons will be provided to the applicants in due course after they receive their certificate.*

*Where an arrangement has been approved, the written reasons are not required to be presented to the ART clinic in order to commence treatment; the clinic only requires the certificate indicating the Panel's approval of the arrangement.*

*8.5 Review of a Panel decision not to approve an arrangement*

*A decision of the Panel not to approve a surrogacy arrangement may be subject to review by the Victorian Civil and Administrative Tribunal (VCAT)[216].*

*An application for review must be made within 28 days after the day on which the Panel's decision is made[217].*

*For further information about applying to the VCAT for a review of a Panel decision, please visit [https://www.vcat.vic.gov.au/privacy-and-health-records/review-of-a-decision-by-the-patient-review-panel](https://www.vcat.vic.gov.au/privacy-and-health-records/review-of-a-decision-by-the-patient-review-panel).*

*7. When is a new approval required?*

*7.1 Same applicants – arrangement to create sibling*

*Where a surrogacy arrangement results in the birth of a child, none of the parties have changed and the applicants wish to enter into a second surrogacy arrangement to have another child, a new approval by the Panel will still be required. However, depending on the length of time since the previous surrogacy arrangement, it is likely that the majority of the material from the original application can be resubmitted as part of the new surrogacy application.*

*However, the following documents would be required:*

a. *an addendum counselling report: it will not be necessary for the addendum counselling report to comprehensively address all of the prescribed matters again. However, at a minimum, it should reflect discussion in the counselling session(s) about any issues that arose during the previous surrogacy arrangement, what impact (if any) the arrangement had on the relationship between all of the relevant parties and how the relinquishment of the child went;*
b. *updated legal advice for the commissioning parent/s and surrogate mother and her partner (if any) to reflect any changes to the law since the prior arrangement;*

215

such as to what a surrogate can be reimbursed for as per the Assisted Reproductive Treatment Regulations 2019, which came into operation on 13 December 2019;
c. if the surrogate had any medical issues with the pregnancy or birth, or post birth, or is now of an advanced maternal age, then a fresh assessment by her doctor as to her suitability and the current risks is requested.

*In some circumstances, the Chairperson may decide that an application for a subsequent arrangement to create a sibling where none of the parties have changed can be considered on the papers and without the applicants having to attend a Panel hearing. However, this would be the exception and is determined on a case-by-case basis at the discretion of the Panel Chairperson. In that case, applicants are still entitled to attend the hearing of their application should they wish to.*

### 7.2 Same commissioning parent/s, change of surrogate

*A completely new application will be required and applicants will be asked to appear before the Panel where there is a new surrogate mother involved in an arrangement, regardless of whether the previous arrangement resulted in the birth of a child or not. Some documentation from the previous arrangement relating to the commissioning parents, such as legal advice, may still be able to be used, provided that it is up-to-date and reflects the current legal requirements. However, applicants will be required to undergo further counselling and psychological assessment. As such, new counselling reports and psychological assessments will need to be completed and should address the implications of the change of surrogate to the proposed arrangement for the other parties.*

### 7.3 Donor joining arrangement or change of donor

*Where a surrogacy arrangement has been approved previously by the Panel, and a subsequent arrangement is proposed where there will be a change to who will be providing the gametes for the embryos, a new approval by the Panel will be required.*

*This will include circumstances such as:*

a. *the commissioning parent/s were previously using embryos formed from their own gametes and have decided to use donor gametes or embryos;*
b. *the commissioning parent/s previously used donor gametes or embryos and have decided to change donor/s;*

*The following documents should be submitted with the new application:*

a. an addendum counselling report: it will not be necessary for the addendum counselling report to comprehensively address all of the prescribed matters again. However, it should at a minimum reflect discussion in the counselling session(s) about any issues that arose during the previous arrangement, and the implications of the new donor on the arrangement and potential future child;
b. updated legal advice (if required) for the commissioning parent/s and surrogate mother and her partner (if any) to reflect any changes to the law since the prior arrangement; such as to what a surrogate can be reimbursed for as per the Assisted Reproductive Treatment Regulations 2019, which came into operation on 13 December 2019;
c. if a donor was not previously part of the arrangement, addendum legal advice will be required by the commissioning parent/s and the surrogate mother and her partner (if any) that addresses the legal implications of using donor gametes if this was not previously covered in earlier legal advice;
d. if the surrogate had any medical issues with the pregnancy or birth, or post birth, or is now of an advanced maternal age, then a fresh assessment by her doctor as to her suitability and the current risks is requested.

*If the new **donor is known** to the applicants, then the Panel will request that all parties appear before it again in order to satisfy itself of the matters it must consider under the ART Act. However, if the new **donor is unknown** to the applicants, then the Panel Chairperson **may** decide that the application can be considered on the papers and without the applicants having to attend a Panel hearing if all other aspects of the application are unchanged.*

*7.4 Same-sex male commissioning parents where embryos created (or intended to be created) from either commissioning parent*

*Where a same-sex male couple enters into a surrogacy arrangement as commissioning parents, either 150commissioning parent may choose to create embryos using their gametes. If both commissioning parents want to create embryos using their gametes, the Panel does **not** require that separate applications be made to the Panel.*

*Instead, a single application can be made that stipulates that embryos will be created using the gametes of both commissioning parents and how a decision will be made about which embryos will be used and when. However, the required counselling and psychological assessments must ensure that all parties to the agreement are aware of this and consent to either parent's gametes being used in the arrangement. For example, the surrogate must be aware of, and consent to, embryos formed from the gametes of either commissioning parent being implanted into her body. Moreover, the Panel must be satisfied that children born as a result of such arrangements are made aware of information about their genetic parents, as stipulated in section 5(c) of the ART Act.*

*Finally, this does not dispense with the need for parties to make a new application to the Panel as outlined in 7.1 above."*

## Commercial surrogacy

Section 44 of the Assisted Reproductive Treatment Act 2008 (Vic)[218] provides:

> *"(1) A surrogate mother must not receive any material benefit or advantage as a result of a surrogacy arrangement.*
>
> *Penalty: 240 penalty units or 2 years imprisonment or both.*
>
> *(2) Subsection (1) does not prevent a surrogate mother being reimbursed for the prescribed costs actually incurred by the surrogate mother as a direct consequence of entering into the surrogacy arrangement.*
>
> *(3) To the extent that a surrogacy arrangement provides for a matter other than the reimbursement for costs actually incurred by the surrogate mother the arrangement is void and unenforceable."*

It can be an offence, both in Victoria and overseas, punishable by up to 15 years imprisonment to pay an egg, sperm or embryo donor a fee. **See chapter 11.**

## Advertising for a surrogate/ advertising seeking intended parents

Section 45 of the Assisted Reproductive Act 2008 (Vic)[219] provides:

> *"(1) A person must not publish, or cause to be published, a statement, advertisement, notice or document—*
>
> > *(a) to the effect that a person is or may be willing to enter into a surrogacy arrangement; or*
> >
> > *(b) to the effect that a person is seeking another person who is or may be willing to enter into a surrogacy arrangement or to act as a surrogate mother or to arrange a surrogacy arrangement; or*
> >
> > *(c) to the effect that the person is or may be willing to arrange a surrogacy arrangement; or*
> >
> > *(d) to the effect that a person is or may be willing to accept any benefit under a surrogacy arrangement, whether for himself or herself or for another person; or*
> >
> > *(e) that is intended or likely to counsel or procure a person to agree to act as a surrogate mother; or*

*(f) to the effect that a person is or may be willing to act as a surrogate mother.*

*Penalty: 240 penalty units or 2 years imprisonment or both.*

*(2) In this section—*

*"publish" means—*

*(a) publish in any newspaper; or*

*(b) publish by means of television, radio or the Internet; or*

*(c) otherwise disseminate to the public."*

While sending an email to someone or posting in a private Facebook group is publish to the Internet- it would appear that the intent of the provision is doing so to the public- and therefore to send an email to someone or to post to a private group on Facebook would be lawful.

## Where are the offences committed?

Only in Victoria.

## What should the budget be for surrogacy in the Victoria?

Aim for $75,000. See chapter 6. **See also chapter 2 as to Medicare.**

## How much can a surrogate be paid in Victoria?

She can only be paid her prescribed costs: regulation 11 *Assisted Reproductive Treatment Regulations 2019* (Vic)[220]. What these are will vary in each case. The prescribed costs are similar to those costs allowed in Queensland, NSW, SA and Tasmania- but are more limited as to loss of earnings.

## Who can access surrogacy in the Victoria?

Anyone. The definition of *commissioning parents* is not limited to two people.

## See chapter 13.

## Where can the medical treatment occur?

The child must be conceived as a result of a procedure carried out in Victoria: section 20 *Status of Children Act 1974* (Vic)[221].

Therefore, it is likely that if the IVF occurs interstate, if the implantation occurs in the ACT, that should be sufficient, but there is no case law on that yet. However, importation of donor gametes and embryos requires the approval of VARTA, and should not be assumed to occur easily.

## Can traditional surrogacy occur?

Not through a clinic: section 40 *Assisted Reproductive Treatment Act 2008* (Vic)[222]. It is lawful to undertake traditional surrogacy at home.

## Does there need to be a genetic link between the parents and child?

No.

## Must the surrogate already have given birth to another child?

Yes: section 4- *Assisted Reproductive Treatment Act 2008* (Vic)[223].

## How old do the intended parents have to be to enter into the surrogacy arrangement?

18 or older: not specified.

## How old do the surrogate and her partner have to be to enter into the surrogacy arrangement?

The surrogate has to be 25 or older: section 40 *Assisted Reproductive Treatment Act 2008* (Vic)[224]. Oddly, there is no age specified for her partner. While in theory someone under 18 could enter into a surrogacy arrangement, under the *Family Law Act 1975* (Cth) that person's parents absent a court order have parental responsibility, then it is clear that the surrogate and her partner have to be 18 or older. It is unclear whether the surrogate's partner can be a party to a lawful surrogacy agreement, although the partner is a parent under the *Status of Children Act 1974* (Vic) and possibly the *Family Law Act 1975* (Cth) so his or her consent to the process would ordinarily be considered necessary.

## Does the surrogacy arrangement need to be written?

No. However, it would be foolish to have an oral agreement. An oral agreement is worth the paper it's written on.

### Does independent legal advice have to be provided before entering into the surrogacy arrangement?

Yes: if through an IVF clinic: section 40 *Assisted Reproductive Treatment Act 2008* (Vic)[225] but not necessarily if traditional surrogacy at home. It would be extremely foolish to enter into a surrogacy arrangement without obtaining independent legal advice first.

### Does counselling need to be obtained before the surrogacy arrangement is entered into?

Only if through an IVF clinic: section 40 Assisted Reproductive Treatment Act 2008 (Vic)[226].

### Who are the parents when the child is born?

The surrogate and her partner: *Status of Children Act 1974* (Vic).

### Who are named on the birth certificate as the parents?

The surrogate and her partner: *Status of Children Act 1974* (Vic).

### Is a post-birth report or counselling required?

No.

### When can the application be made to the Court for a parentage order?

Ordinarily between when the baby is 28 days and 6 months old: section 20 *Status of Children Act 1974* (Vic)[227].

### Which court makes the parentage order?

The Supreme Court or County Court of Victoria: section 18 *Status of Children Act 2008* (Vic)[228]. Typically, applications are made to the County Court.

### Do we have to physically go to court?

Yes, subject to Covid.

### Can the baby go to court?

Yes.

### Can photos be taken in the court?

Yes. One judge loved having her photo taken with the parents, children, surrogate and partner. The child would receive a teddy bear from the local Lions Club. It is a very warm approach. I wish it were the norm across the country.

## Are the intended parents then the parents for the purposes of Australian law?

Yes: section 60HB *Family Law Act 1975* (Cth), regulation 12CAA *Family Law Regulations 1984* (Cth)- **see chapter 28 interstate arrangements**.

## Have I acted for clients in Victoria about surrogacy?

Yes. My first surrogacy client in Victoria was in 2008, before the commencement of the *Assisted Reproductive Treatment Act 2008* (Vic).

[209] http://www.austlii.edu.au/cgi-bin/viewdb/au/legis/vic/consol_act/arta2008360/

[210] http://www.austlii.edu.au/cgi-bin/viewdb/au/legis/vic/consol_reg/artr2019469/

[211] http://www.austlii.edu.au/cgi-bin/viewdb/au/legis/vic/consol_act/soca1974199/

[212] Details as to who the Panel considers an "independent psychologist" for its purposes are set out on p10.

[213] In this context, the Panel notes Recommendation 9 of Helping Victorians create families with assisted reproductive treatment - Final Report of Independent Review of Assisted Reproductive Treatment (the Gorton Review) which includes the recommendation that the ART Act be amended to remove the requirement for same-sex couples to demonstrate that they are unlikely to become pregnant.

[214] JS and LS v Patient Review Panel [2011] VCAT 856 at paragraph 14.

[215] JS and LS v Patient Review Panel [2011] VCAT 856.

[216] Assisted Reproductive Treatment Act 2008 (Vic), s 96(b).

[217] Assisted Reproductive Treatment Act 2008 (Vic), s 98.

[218] http://www.austlii.edu.au/cgi-bin/viewdoc/au/legis/vic/consol_act/arta2008360/s44.html

[219] http://www.austlii.edu.au/cgi-bin/viewdoc/au/legis/vic/consol_act/arta2008360/s45.html

[220] http://www.austlii.edu.au/cgi-bin/viewdoc/au/legis/qld/consol_act/sa2010139/s11.html

[221] http://www.austlii.edu.au/cgi-bin/viewdoc/au/legis/vic/consol_act/soca1974199/s20.html

[222] http://www.austlii.edu.au/cgi-bin/viewdoc/au/legis/vic/consol_act/arta2008360/s40.html

[223] http://www.austlii.edu.au/cgi-bin/viewdoc/au/legis/vic/consol_act/arta2008360/s40.html

[224] http://www.austlii.edu.au/cgi-bin/viewdoc/au/legis/vic/consol_act/arta2008360/s40.html

[225] http://www.austlii.edu.au/cgi-bin/viewdoc/au/legis/vic/consol_act/arta2008360/s40.html

[226] http://www.austlii.edu.au/cgi-bin/viewdoc/au/legis/vic/consol_act/arta2008360/s40.html

[227] http://www.austlii.edu.au/cgi-bin/viewdoc/au/legis/vic/consol_act/soca1974199/s20.html

[228] http://www.austlii.edu.au/cgi-bin/viewdoc/au/legis/vic/consol_act/soca1974199/s18.html

CHAPTER 27

# SURROGACY IN WESTERN AUSTRALIA

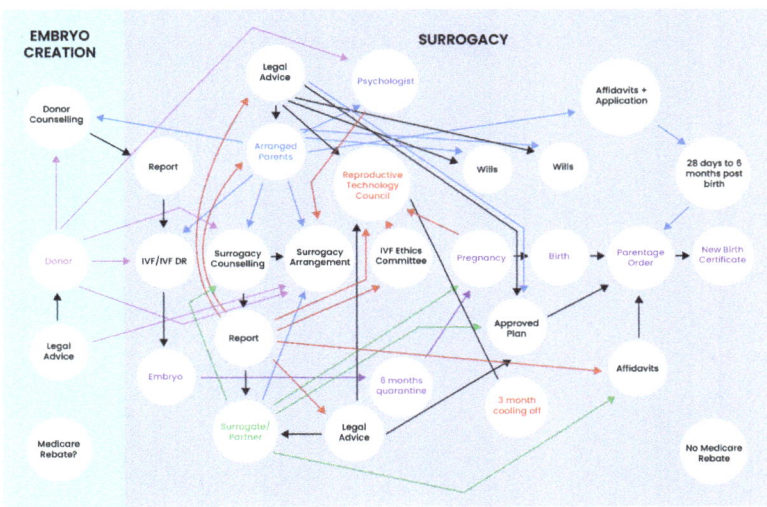

The *Surrogacy Act 2008* (WA) regulates altruistic surrogacy, but criminalises commercial surrogacy. Surrogacy is also regulated by regulations and by the *Human Reproductive Technology Act 1991* (WA).

The surrogacy arrangement must be approved by the State regulator, the Reproductive Technology Council of WA. Approval is required before treatment can commence. Western Australia, Victoria, New Zealand and Israel are the only places in the world that require State sanction of surrogacy arrangements before intended parents can proceed.

Surrogacy is not allowed in WA for single men or gay couples. **See chapter 13**.

In the 12 years since the enactment of the *Surrogacy Act 2008* (WA) up to 30 June 2020, there had been a total of 15 children born, or just over 1 a year[229]. By contrast, if the number of Australian children born overseas per head of population was the same in WA as the rest of the country, then the number of children born overseas to Western Australian residents in the years ended 30 June 2019, 2020 and 2021, the respective figures would be 23, 27 and 22. WA has approximately 10% of the Australian population. **See chapter 10**.

## Estimated proportion of domestic v international surrogacy births in WA for the year ended 30 June 2019

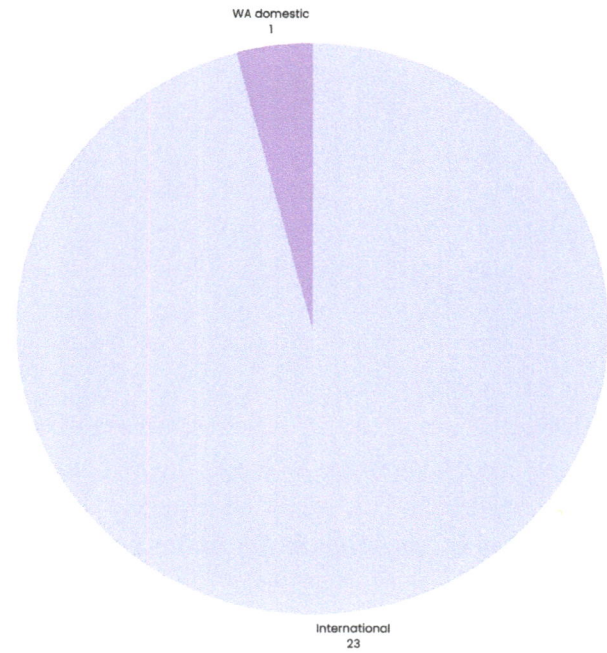

## Commercial surrogacy

Section 8 of the *Surrogacy Act 2008* (WA) provides:

> "*A person who enters into a surrogacy arrangement that is for reward commits an offence.*
>
> *Penalty: a fine of $24 000 or imprisonment for 2 years."*

"*Surrogacy arrangement that is for reward*" is defined in section 6 of the *Surrogacy Act 2008* (WA)[231]:

> "*(1) This Part refers to a surrogacy arrangement as being for reward if the arrangement provides for any person to*

*receive any payment or valuable consideration other than for reasonable expenses associated with —*

*(a) the pregnancy or the birth; or*

*(b) any assessment or expert advice in connection with the arrangement.*

*(2) Reasonable expenses associated with achieving, or attempting to achieve, the pregnancy are reasonable expenses associated with the pregnancy.*

*(3) An expense is a reasonable expense for the purposes of subsection (1)(a) to the extent only that it is —*

*(a) a reasonable medical expense that is not recoverable under any health insurance or other scheme; or*

*(b) the value of earnings foregone because of leave taken —*

*(i) for a period of not more than 2 months during which the birth occurs or was expected to occur; or*

*(ii) at any other time for medical reasons arising during the pregnancy;*

*or*

*(c) a reasonable expense of psychological counselling; or*

*(d) a premium payable for health, disability or life insurance that —*

*(i) would not have been taken out if the surrogacy arrangement had not been entered into; and*

*(ii) provides cover for a period during which an expense referred to in another paragraph of this subsection is incurred or might be, or have been expected to be, incurred."*

It can be an offence, both in WA and overseas, punishable by up to 15 years imprisonment to pay an egg, sperm or embryo donor a fee. **See chapter 11**.

**WARNING: Anyone living in Western Australia considering undertaking a surrogacy arrangement interstate or overseas should not be obtaining advice from a Western Australian lawyer. I note that I have called for the repeal of this provision, but it remains.**

Section 11 of the *Surrogacy Act 2008* (WA)[232] provides:

*"(1) A person who provides a service knowing that the service is to facilitate a surrogacy arrangement that is for reward commits a crime except in the circumstances described in subsection (2).*

*(2) It is not an offence against subsection (1) if the service is a health service provided to the birth mother after she has become pregnant.*

*Penalty: imprisonment for 5 years.*

*Summary conviction penalty: a fine of $12 000 or imprisonment for one year."*

## Advertising for a surrogate/ advertising seeking intended parents

Section 10 of the *Surrogacy Act 2008* (WA)[233] provides:

*"A person commits an offence if the person publishes or causes to be published —*

*(a) anything that is intended to, or likely to, induce a person to enter into a surrogacy arrangement that is for reward; or*

*(b) anything to the effect that a person who is willing to enter into a surrogacy arrangement that is for reward is sought; or*

*(c) anything to the effect that a person is or might be willing to enter into a surrogacy arrangement that is for reward.*

*Penalty: a fine of $6 000."*

On the face of it, to advertise for an altruistic surrogate is lawful. However, because the expenses in WA that are allowed are so restrictive (for example, although it is the largest state, it is illegal to pay for the surrogate's travel), to advertise may be committing an offence. Get advice first.

## Where are the offences committed?

In WA or anywhere else if elements of the offence occur in WA: s.12 *Criminal Code 1913* (WA). Therefore, if a WA resident enters in WA into a Canadian surrogacy arrangement, the WA resident is almost certainly committing an offence under the Surrogacy Act. Canadian surrogacy agreements, which are altruistic, always make allowance for travel and for snow shovelling costs- neither of which are allowed in WA, but would be allowed under equivalent laws in ACT, Qld, NSW, SA, even though their laws can also extend overseas. WA residents must obtain advice early- but cannot do so from a WA lawyer!

## What should the budget be for surrogacy in WA?

Aim for $80,000. **See chapter 6. See also chapter 2 as to Medicare**.

## How much can a surrogate be paid in WA?

These are quite restrictive, as I have set out above. What these are will vary in each case.

## Who can access surrogacy in WA?

Heterosexual couples, lesbian couples and single women but not single males or a male couples: section 19 Surrogacy Act 2008 (WA)[234]. **See chapter 13**. It is not clear how transgender, intersex and non-binary people would be treated.

## Where can the medical treatment occur?

Treatment must be in WA.

## Can traditional surrogacy occur?

Yes.

## Does there need to be a genetic link between the parents and child?

No. Uniquely in the world, Western Australia requires that any genetic donor and their partner must be a party to the surrogacy arrangement and accordingly must receive legal advice and counselling: section 17 *Surrogacy Act 2008* (WA)[235]. This limits the use of clinic recruited donors who may not be known to the parties, and therefore restricts the availability of surrogacy in WA.

## Does the surrogate have to have given birth already to another child?

Yes, unless there are exceptional circumstances: section *17 Surrogacy Act 2008* (WA)[236].

## How old do the intended parents have to be to enter into the surrogacy arrangement?

One of them has to be 25 by the time of applying to court: section 19 Surrogacy Act 2008 (WA)[237].

## How old do the surrogate and her partner have to be to enter into the surrogacy arrangement?

Section 17 of the *Surrogacy Act 2008* (WA)[238] requires the surrogate to be 25, but is silent about the age of the partner. While in theory someone under 18 could enter into a surrogacy arrangement, under the *Family Law Act 1975* (Cth) that person's parents absent a court order have parental responsibility, then it is clear that the surrogate and her partner have to be 18 or older.

## Does the surrogacy arrangement need to be written?

Yes: section 17 *Surrogacy Act 2008* (WA)[239].

## Does independent legal advice have to be provided before entering into the surrogacy arrangement?

Yes: section 17, *Surrogacy Act 2008* (WA)[240].

## Does counselling need to be obtained before the surrogacy arrangement is entered into?

Yes, with two counsellors, and there is a minimum 3 month cooling off period before the application is dealt with by the Reproductive Technology Council: section 17, *Surrogacy Act 2008* (WA)[241].

## Who are the parents when the child is born?

The surrogate and her partner: *Parentage Act 2004* (ACT).

## Who are named on the birth certificate as the parents?

The surrogate and her partner: *Parentage Act 2004* (ACT).

## Is a post-birth report or counselling required?
No.

## When can the application be made to the Court for a parentage order?
Ordinarily between when the baby is 28 days and 6 months old: section 20 Surrogacy Act 2008 (ACT)[242].

## Which court makes the parentage order?
The Family Court of Western Australia: section 14 Surrogacy Act 2008 (WA).

## Do we have to physically go to court?
Yes, subject to Covid.

## Can the baby go to court?
Check with the court.

## Can photos be taken in the court?
Check with the court.

## Are the intended parents then the parents for the purposes of Australian law?
Yes: section 60HB *Family Law Act 1975* (Cth), regulation 12CAA *Family Law Regulations 1984* (Cth)- except if the child is born in Victoria- see chapter 28 interstate arrangements.

## Have I acted for clients in Western Australia about surrogacy?
Yes. My first surrogacy clients in Western Australia were in about 2011.

[229] Annual report of the Reproductive Technology Council of Western Australia for the year ended 30 June 2020 discloses, consistent with previous reports of the Council, that the total number of births from surrogacy up to 30 June 2019 was 15. The annual report for the year ending 30 June 2020 says as to the number of surrogacy arrangements that have been approved, but is silent as to the number of births, from which it can be inferred that up to 30 June 2020 that total of 15 had not increased. The reports can be found here: https://www.rtc.org.au/annual-reports/

[230] The most recent year for domestic births via surrogacy in WA.

[231] http://www.austlii.edu.au/cgi-bin/viewdoc/au/legis/wa/consol_act/sa2008139/s6.html

[232] http://www.austlii.edu.au/cgi-bin/viewdoc/au/legis/wa/consol_act/sa2008139/s11.html

[233] http://www.austlii.edu.au/cgi-bin/viewdoc/au/legis/wa/consol_act/sa2008139/s10.html

[234] http://www.austlii.edu.au/cgi-bin/viewdoc/au/legis/wa/consol_act/sa2008139/s19.html

[235] http://www.austlii.edu.au/cgi-bin/viewdoc/au/legis/wa/consol_act/sa2008139/s17.html

[236] http://www.austlii.edu.au/cgi-bin/viewdoc/au/legis/wa/consol_act/sa2008139/s17.html

[237] http://www.austlii.edu.au/cgi-bin/viewdoc/au/legis/wa/consol_act/sa2008139/s19.html

[238] http://www.austlii.edu.au/cgi-bin/viewdoc/au/legis/wa/consol_act/sa2008139/s17.html

[239] http://www.austlii.edu.au/cgi-bin/viewdoc/au/legis/wa/consol_act/sa2008139/s17.html

[240] http://www.austlii.edu.au/cgi-bin/viewdoc/au/legis/wa/consol_act/sa2008139/s17.html

[241] http://www.austlii.edu.au/cgi-bin/viewdoc/au/legis/wa/consol_act/sa2008139/s17.html

[242] http://www.austlii.edu.au/cgi-bin/viewdoc/au/legis/wa/consol_act/sa2008139/s20.html

## CHAPTER 28

# INTERSTATE ARRANGEMENTS

As can be seen from **chapters 20 to 27**, the legal landscape regulating surrogacy across Australia while similar in intent varies in fine detail- which can then make planning interstate surrogacy arrangements quite difficult and time consuming at times. I sought when I gave evidence to the 2015 House of Representatives surrogacy inquiry that there either be national laws, or at least uniform state and territory laws. Despite the Committee calling for such an approach in its report in 2016, six years later little has happened.

There have been changes in South Australia and Victoria, which have meant, following representations made by others and me, that the issue of surrogates' expenses is more uniform.

However, there are clear anomalies. This means that if the intended parents live in say NSW and the surrogate and her partner live in WA, not only will the surrogacy arrangement have to comply with NSW law, it must also not result in the committing of a criminal offence in WA. Under NSW law, for example, it is lawful to reimburse the surrogate for the cost of massages, or acupuncture, or to pay for her reasonable travel or accommodation. To do any of those in WA is a criminal offence.

Because the Northern Territory does not have laws about surrogacy, but there have been surrogates from the Top End, great care and planning must be put into where she gives birth (and how she gets there). If a surrogate gave birth in the Top End it might be impossible to effect a transfer of parentage to the intended parents. The surrogate therefore has to fly – usually by 28 weeks- and then be provided accommodation and the necessities of life until she gives birth in say Melbourne, or endure a very long drive across the Outback, where she has the risk of something going wrong and giving birth or having a miscarriage miles form any medical help.

While federal legislation, the Family Law Act 1975 (Cth) and the Evidence Act 1995 (Cth) and section 118 of the Commonwealth Constitution make plain what is obvious in a federation- that court orders made in one State would be recognised in other states, and that parents of a child by virtue of a parentage order made by a court in one state are parents of that child right across Australia- that's not good enough for Victoria. Victoria insists under its *Status of Children Act 1974* (Vic) that if a child is the subject of a parentage order made interstate, but the child is born in Victoria, then the parents have to also obtain a registration order form a Victorian court in order to show them on the birth certificate as the parents.

Aside from the fact that this process is likely to fail any constitutional test, by requiring parents to show that they are the parents and worthy of having a registration order made in their favour, they are being subjected to:

- Yet another court proceeding, when they should be trying to catch up on sleep while they have a baby who is giving them sleepless nights.
- The stress of, yet again, having to prove that they are good enough to be parents, when they should never have had to do so.
- Delay before they are formally recognised on their child's birth certificates as the parents, which has practical effects, including in some case obtaining a Medicare card for the child.
- Likely another $10,000 or so in legal fees for having to make the application, instead of being able to spend that money on their child's direct needs.

# CHAPTER 29

# SURROGACY ISSUES FOR AUSTRALIANS LIVING OVERSEAS

When I first acted for overseas surrogacy clients in about 2008, I did not expect to act for clients about ART who lived in 34 countries overseas- **see chapter 1**. However, my experience has enabled me to boil down their needs to some basics.

Australians living overseas who seek to become parents through surrogacy have to consider a number of factors:

- Do (or can) they undertake surrogacy overseas either in the country they live in, or some other country?
- Do they instead pursue surrogacy back in Australia? Assuming they have a surrogate back home, they are likely to have to move home to do so. However, there are different rules that apply about jurisdiction in the various Australian states, so there can be some flexibility with this, depending on where they go.
- Assuming they undertake surrogacy in some place other than where they live, is it legal for them to do so? Australian residents in Hong Kong, for example, who pursue commercial surrogacy outside of Hong Kong (there is none available in Hong Kong) commit an offence in Hong Kong.
- Might they committing an offence under Australian law by pursuing surrogacy where they live or in some other place? This can happen inadvertently by payment of egg donors or surrogates from Australian bank accounts, or because one or both of them is domiciled in NSW, despite living overseas. **See chapter 11**.
- What process is involved in bringing the baby back home to where they live? What if it doesn't work? What is their back up plan? *There must always be a back up plan*. This became obvious during the pandemic. Clients

of mine who lived in Singapore and China, for example, were not able to take their children back there- when they were doing surrogacy in the US. Instead, they had to come back to Australia with their children- even though they did not live here.
- Do they have other citizenships, and if so do they want their child to hold those citizenships (in which case I would refer my clients to other lawyers in those countries) or only Australian citizenship?
- Where are the embryos? Just because they have created embryos overseas does not mean they can be used here. The rules are strict. Just as laws across the country are not always compatible, so too with international laws and practice in this space. However, if planning is put into the process at the beginning, with suitable advice, the answer is yes. As I have said elsewhere, prevention is better than cure.

Of course, some of these issues don't apply just to Australian intended parents living overseas- but also to many Australians living in Australia- but these issues can be more pronounced and urgent for expatriates.

## CHAPTER 30

# PLAYING NICELY WITH OTHERS

As a child, I would regularly play chess with my dad. Much as Mitch wants to play chess with me, I won't. My reluctance is like that of many lawyers. We are highly competitive and don't like to lose.

I mention chess, however, because it teaches skills of thinking three or more steps ahead, which is vital in this space.

To do this job well, and get intended parents in and out of their surrogacy journey as quickly as possible, I try to play nicely with others. The process is a collaboration- working as necessary with other professionals, including doctors, IVF clinics, counsellors and other lawyers to try and help these people become parents. Each have our own roles to play and our own duties- but when we act in a collaborative manner, we are more likely to achieve results for our clients that are cheaper, quicker and less stressful for them.

In the process I have been lucky to have learnt many ways of doing things better for my clients. Surrogacy is in essence a transparent process built on trust. The intended parents trust the surrogate and she in turn trusts them. When it comes to medical information, for example, having absolute clarity is essential for trust.

When there are particularly difficult problems, I like to problem solve. Left to myself, I will get a writing pad and a pen, stare out the window and look at some clouds, and then write down the possible solution. There have been many times when in the process of brainstorming like that I have come up with a solution that no one else had considered- and it fixed the problem. Too many of us are linear thinkers. Lateral thinking is often required to solve these complex problems.

When I am not able to solve the problem all by myself, I call in others. During the pandemic, for example, a client of mine was overseas with his baby, and was stressed that he could not get home. There were a series of hurdles that had to be jumped, and each one seemed to be getting bigger each day, courtesy of Covid. He was stressed. He had done nothing wrong, except to be in the wrong place at the wrong time.

My client and baby were able to return home. I made sure that the lawyer over there, plus a migration agent here and me all had (as it turns out a couple of calls) a three way call to problem solve. The process worked. By workshopping it, and sharing our views, any barriers between us melted away, and a plan for action was undertaken- successfully.

Surrogacy is simply the most complex way to reproduce. Sometimes the bits don't work. Playing nicely with others, I have found, helps problem solve and lets my clients become parents sooner with less stress, delay and cost than might otherwise have been the case.

## CHAPTER 31

# A CALL FOR CHANGE

If there were any doubt, the statistics in **Chapters 10** and **27** show that Australians are voting with their feet and going overseas for surrogacy, despite bans in most places not to engage in commercial surrogacy overseas.

The bans don't work. They are difficult to enforce, and the political will has not been there to prosecute, which brings the law into disrepute.

We should be honest and admit that while lawyers like me, and doctors, counsellors, nurses, embryologists, and judges are all getting paid in the process- the extraordinary women, surrogates, who take all the risk (including the risks of death and injury) to help others, are the *only* ones not getting paid. As a result, we have too few surrogacy journeys for the size of our country, and we continue to export our intended parents overseas.

Efforts to stop intended parents going overseas will not work. All intended parents have to do is to look at their phone, either via Google or WeChat, and discover that they can indeed become parents- and can do so now. Whether that is a wise way of choosing a surrogacy agency is beside the point. It's reality. Digital disruption is not confined to Uber. To quote Sir David Attenborough again:

> *"So animals and ourselves, to continue the line, will endure all kinds of hardship, overcome all kinds of difficulties, and eventually the next generation appears."*

It has been suggested that a way to prevent Australian intended parents undertaking commercial surrogacy overseas is to prevent the children returning until the parents can convince some Australian authority, like a court, that they complied with Australian policies. Such an approach could render the children Stateless, victimising the weak and innocent- and would be in breach of Australia's obligations under various conventions including the *International Convention on the Rights of the*

*Child.* The experience in the UK where judges are required to authorise recognition of the parents as the parents, is that they always do. What's the point?

I love it when my clients do surrogacy in Australia. If they can undertake surrogacy here, all the better. I would rather they did surrogacy locally than have to go overseas. After all that's how I became a dad through surrogacy. We have good (but not perfect) systems, though we should have automatic recognition of intended parents at birth- **see chapter 2**, excellent IVF clinics, excellent fertility counsellors, a great human rights framework, and above all an independent judiciary to oversee the lot. Basically, we've got the lot, that's what- except we don't pay a reasonable amount to those who are pregnant, have morning sickness and bloated feet, and take the risk, do the heavy lifting and have the pain of giving birth.

Our efforts should be focussed on properly compensating women for the pain and suffering of being pregnant and giving birth – and the related risk of death or injury, these being Australian women who will have the benefit of good medical care, great hospitals, counselling, independent legal advice and human rights protection marked by the rule of law. This is a more practical approach than the one we have where with a population of about one third of the UK's, the number of children born overseas via surrogacy is about the same in absolute numbers each year[243] at about 200 here and 200 in the UK.

Too many of our overseas surrogacy journeys are to places where quality IVF is poor and the human rights frameworks for surrogates are poor, non-existent, or in the words of a retired judge, *"the Wild West, where anything goes"*[244].

We can do better.

At the time of writing these words, Thailand is now considering strict laws to regulate commercial surrogacy. Thailand has realised that banning commercial surrogacy doesn't work. Thailand has made this decision in order to reduce the trafficking of women and children.

While there has not been the trafficking of women and children in Australia with surrogacy, we too can grasp the nettle and decide to make changes to enable more surrogacy to be undertaken at home than abroad. After all, if the Americans can undertake surrogacy successfully, why can't we?

---

[243] According to my colleague Natalie Gamble in the UK, about 200 children are born overseas via surrogacy to UK citizens each year, which is about the same number for Australians, as seen in chapter 10.

[244] The Hon. John Pascoe AC, CVO, former Chief Justice of the Family Court of Australia.

www.ingramcontent.com/pod-product-compliance
Lightning Source LLC
Chambersburg PA
CBHW040240010526
44107CB00065B/2816